KNITTING FOR HIM

KNITTING
FOR HIM

27 classic projects to keep him warm

Martin Storey
& Wendy Baker

PHOTOGRAPHY BY
John Heseltine

The Taunton Press

The Taunton Press
Inspiration for hands-on living®

The Taunton Press
63 South Main St. PO Box 5506
Newtown, CT 06470-5506
www.taunton.com

First published in 2007 by Rowan Yarns

Editor Susan Berry
Designer Anne Wilson
Photographer John Heseltine
Stylist Emma Freemantle
Pattern writers Sue Whiting and Penny Hill
Pattern checkers Stella Smith
Diagrams Stella Smith

Associate Publisher Susan Berry

Library of Congress Cataloging-in-Publication Data

Storey, Martin, 1958-
   Knitting for him : 27 classic projects to keep him warm /
Martin Storey & Wendy Baker ; photography by John
Heseltine.
      p. cm.
   ISBN 978-1-56158-992-0
   1. Knitting—Patterns. 2. Men's clothing. I. Baker, Wendy,
1961- II. Title.
TT820.S865 2007
746.43'2041—dc22

                                        2007020491

Reproduced and printed in Singapore

CONTENTS

INTRODUCTION

When we were asked to design a collection of hand knits for men for Rowan, we realized that most men prefer garments that are comfortable, above all, and prefer colors that are not too "gaudy." However, in the main, it will be their womenfolk who will knit the patterns in this book, and knitters like interesting stitch and color combinations to work with.

We hope that we have struck the right note in this book: classic but with a contemporary twist. There are certainly a few patterns in this collection that will provide something for more advanced knitters to get their teeth into, as well as quite a few for those who are relatively new to the game.

The yarns chosen are all Rowan's tried and tested classics in standard weights, which knit up well and hold their shape. While some like the Alpaca and Cashsoft ranges are exquisitely soft, others, such as Scottish Tweed are robust, so there is a wide spectrum to choose from.

We hope that you enjoy knitting them and the men in your life appreciate wearing them. It was great fun to create a collection just for men, because their interests tend to get forgotten in the great scheme of things in knitwear. Yet almost every man has a "favorite" sweater in his closet that is worn until (and sometime after) it is full of holes; we hope some of these will achieve a similar longevity!

Our photographer, John Heseltine, shot the garments on location in Ilfracombe, north Devon, which is famous for having a beautiful coastline and the stunning moorland of Exmoor close by. The "natural outdoors" element seemed right for the designs, the natural yarns, and the relaxed style of most of the garments. We hope you agree.

Martin Storey and *Wendy Baker*

CABLE JACKET

Martin Storey

To fit chest

40	42	44	46	48	in
102	107	112	117	122	cm

Finished measurements

AROUND CHEST

49¼	50¾	52¾	54¼	56	in
125	129	134	138	142	cm

LENGTH TO BACK NECK

28	28¼	28¾	29	29½	in
71	72	73	74	75	cm

SLEEVE SEAM

20¾	20¾	21¼	21¼	21½	in
53	53	54	54	55	cm

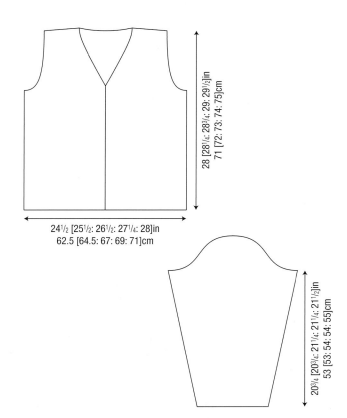

28 [28¼: 28¾: 29: 29½]in
71 [72: 73: 74: 75]cm

24½ [25½: 26½: 27¼: 28]in
62.5 [64.5: 67: 69: 71]cm

20¾ [20¾: 21¼: 21¼: 21½]in
53 [53: 54: 54: 55]cm

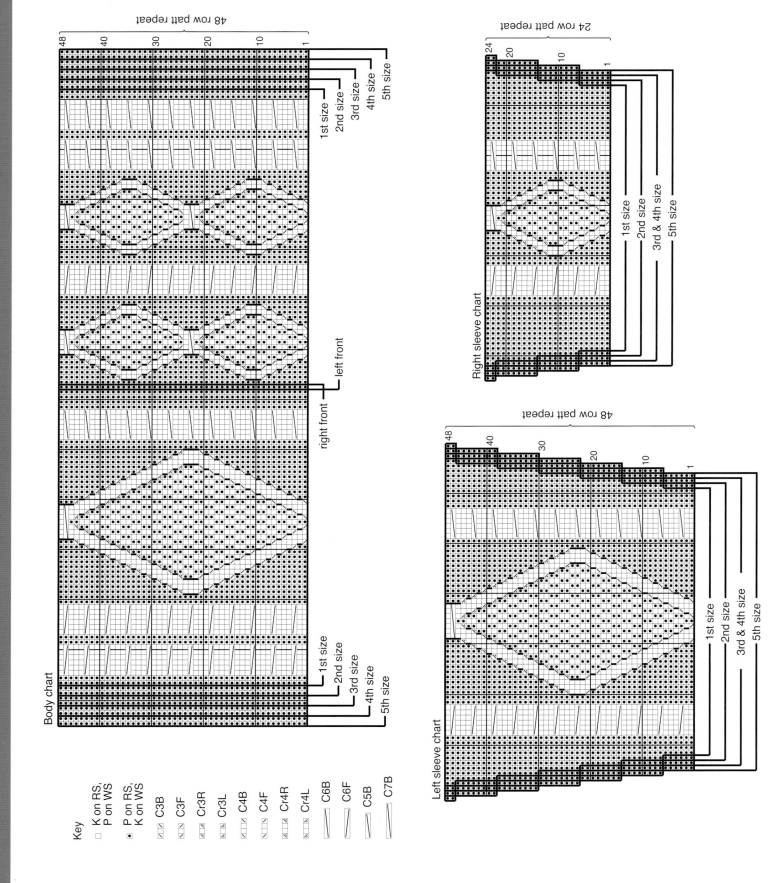

Body chart

Key
□ K on RS, P on WS
● P on RS, K on WS

C3B
C3F
Cr3R
Cr3L
C4B
C4F
Cr4R
Cr4L
C6B
C6F
C5B
C7B

Right sleeve chart

Left sleeve chart

48 row patt repeat

24 row patt repeat

48 row patt repeat

1st size
2nd size
3rd size
4th size
5th size

left front

right front

1st size
2nd size
3rd size
4th size
5th size

1st size
2nd size
3rd & 4th size
5th size

1st size
2nd size
3rd & 4th size
5th size

YARNS

11 (12: 12: 13: 13) x 100g/3½oz balls of Rowan *Scottish Tweed Aran* in Indigo 031

NEEDLES

Pair of size 6 (4mm) knitting needles
Pair of size 8 (5mm) knitting needles
Cable needle

EXTRAS

6 buttons

GAUGE

19 sts and 23 rows to 4in/10cm measured over patt, 16 sts and 23 rows to 4in/10cm measured over rev St st, both using size 8 (5mm) needles *or size to obtain correct gauge.*

ABBREVIATIONS

See page 133.

SPECIAL ABBREVIATIONS

C3B = slip next st onto cable needle and leave at back of work, K2, then K1 from cable needle; **C3F** = slip next 2 sts onto cable needle and leave at front of work, K1, then K2 from cable needle; **Cr3R** = slip next st onto cable needle and leave at back of work, K2, then P1 from cable needle; **Cr3L** = slip next 2 sts onto cable needle and leave at front of work, P1, then K2 from cable needle; **C4B** = slip next st onto cable needle and leave at back of work, K3, then K1 from cable needle; **C4F** = slip next 3 sts onto cable needle and leave at front of work, K1, then K3 from cable needle; **Cr4R** = slip next st onto cable needle and leave at back of work, K3, then P1 from cable needle; **Cr4L** = slip next 3 sts onto cable needle and leave at front of work, P1, then K3 from cable needle; **C5B** = slip next 3 sts onto cable needle and leave at back of work, K2, then K3 from cable needle; **C6B** = slip next 3 sts onto cable needle and leave at back of work, K3, then K3 from cable needle; **C6F** = slip next 3 sts onto cable needle and leave at front of work, K3, then K3 from cable needle; **C7B** = slip next 4 sts onto cable needle and leave at back of work, K3, then K4 from cable needle.

BACK

Using size 6 (4mm) needles, cast on 100 (104: 108: 112: 116) sts.
Row 1 (RS) P0 (0: 1: 0: 0), K1 (0: 1: 1: 0), *P2, K1; rep from * to last 0 (2: 1: 0: 2) sts, P0 (2: 1: 0: 2).
Row 2 K0 (0: 1: 0: 0), P1 (0: 1: 1: 0), *K2, P1; rep from * to last 0 (2: 1: 0: 2) sts, K0 (2: 1: 0: 2).
These 2 rows form rib.
Work in rib for 7 rows more, ending with WS facing for next row.
Row 10 (WS) Rib 2 (4: 6: 8: 10), M1, rib 4, M1, rib 2, M1, rib 4, M1, rib 12, [M1, rib 3] twice, M1, rib 12, M1, rib 4, M1, rib 10, M1, rib 5, M1, rib 6, M1, rib 4, M1, rib 6, M1, rib 5, M1, rib 6, M1, rib 4, M1, rib 2, M1, rib 4, M1, rib to end. 119 (123: 127: 131: 135) sts.
Change to size 8 (5mm) needles.
Starting and ending rows as indicated and repeating the 48 row patt repeat throughout, now work in patt from chart for Body until Back measures 18½in/47cm from cast-on edge, ending with RS facing for next row.

Shape armholes

Keeping patt correct, bind off 8 sts at beg of next 2 rows. 103 (107: 111: 115: 119) sts.
Dec 1 st at each end of next 3 rows, then on foll 3 (4: 5: 6: 7) alt rows, then on 2 foll 4th rows. 87 (89: 91: 93: 95) sts.
Work even until armhole measures 9½ (9¾: 10¼: 10½: 11)in/24 (25: 26: 27: 28)cm, ending with RS facing for next row.

Shape shoulders and back neck

Bind off 8 (9: 9: 9: 9) sts at beg of next 2 rows. 71 (71: 73: 75: 77) sts.
Next row (RS) Bind off 8 (9: 9: 9: 9) sts, patt until there are 13 (12: 12: 13: 13) sts on right needle and turn, leaving rem sts on a holder.
Work each side of neck separately.
Bind off 4 sts at beg of next row.
Bind off rem 9 (8: 8: 9: 9) sts.
With RS facing, rejoin yarn to rem sts, bind off center 29 (29: 31: 31: 33) sts, patt to end.
Complete to match first side, reversing shapings.

POCKET LININGS (make 2)

Using size 8 (5mm) needles, cast on 25 sts.
Starting with a K row, work in St st for 35 rows, ending with WS facing for next row.

Row 36 (WS) [P4, M1] 5 times, P5. 30 sts.
Break off yarn and leave sts on a holder.

LEFT FRONT

Using size 6 (4mm) needles, cast on 50 (52: 54: 56: 58) sts.
Row 1 (RS) P0 (0: 1: 0: 0), K1 (0: 1: 1: 0), *P2, K1; rep from * to last 4 sts, P4.
Row 2 K4, P1, *K2, P1; rep from * to last 0 (2: 1: 0: 2) sts, K0 (2: 1: 0: 2).
These 2 rows form rib.
Work in rib for 7 rows more, ending with WS facing for next row.
Row 10 (WS) Rib 6, M1, rib 5, M1, rib 6, M1, rib 4, M1, rib 6, M1, rib 5, M1, rib 6, M1, rib 4, M1, rib 2, M1, rib 4,

M1, rib to end. 60 (62: 64: 66: 68) sts.
Change to size 8 (5mm) needles.
Starting and ending rows as indicated, now work in patt from chart for Body for 36 rows, ending with RS facing for next row.
Place pocket
Next row (RS) Patt 16 (18: 20: 22: 24) sts, slip next 30 sts onto a holder and, in their place, patt across 30 sts of first Pocket Lining, patt to end.
Cont in patt until Left Front matches Back to start of armhole shaping, ending with RS facing for next row.
Shape armhole
Keeping patt correct, bind off 8 sts at beg of next row. 52 (54: 56: 58: 60) sts.
Work 1 row.
Dec 1 st at armhole edge of next 2 rows, ending with RS facing for next row. 50 (52: 54: 56: 58) sts.
Shape front slope
Keeping patt correct, dec 1 st at armhole edge of next and foll 3 (4: 5: 6: 7) alt rows, then on 2 foll 4th rows **and at the same time** dec 1 st at front slope edge of next and every foll alt row. 36 sts.
Dec 1 st at front slope edge **only** on 2nd and foll 6 (4: 4: 2: 2) alt rows, then on every foll 4th row until 25 (26: 26: 27: 27) sts rem.
Work even until Left Front matches Back to start of shoulder shaping, ending with RS facing for next row.
Shape shoulder
Bind off 8 (9: 9: 9: 9) sts at beg of next and foll alt row.
Work 1 row.
Bind off rem 9 (8: 8: 9: 9) sts.

RIGHT FRONT

Using size 6 (4mm) needles, cast on 50 (52: 54: 56: 58) sts.
Row 1 (RS) P4, K1, *P2, K1; rep from * to last 0 (2: 1: 0: 2) sts, P0 (2: 1: 0: 2).
Row 2 K0 (0: 1: 0: 0), P1 (0: 1: 1: 0), *K2, P1; rep from * to last 4 sts, K4.
These 2 rows form rib.
Work in rib for 7 rows more, ending with WS facing for next row.
Row 10 (WS) Rib 2 (4: 6: 8: 10), M1, rib 4, M1, rib 2, M1, rib 4, M1, rib 12, [M1, rib 3] twice, M1, rib 12, M1, rib 4, M1, rib 4, inc in last st. 60 (62: 64: 66: 68) sts.
Change to size 8 (5mm) needles.

Starting and ending rows as indicated, now work in patt from chart for Body for 36 rows, ending with RS facing for next row.

Place pocket

Next row (RS) Patt 14 sts, slip next 30 sts onto a holder and, in their place, patt across 30 sts of second Pocket Lining, patt to end.

Complete to match Left Front, reversing shapings.

LEFT SLEEVE

Using size 6 (4mm) needles, cast on 46 (48: 50: 50: 52) sts.

Row 1 (RS) P0 (1: 2: 2: 0), *K1, P2; rep from * to last 1 (2: 0: 0: 1) sts, K1 (1: 0: 0: 1), P0 (1: 0: 0: 0).

Row 2 K0 (1: 2: 2: 0), *P1, K2; rep from * to last 1 (2: 0: 0: 1) sts, P1 (1: 0: 0: 1), K0 (1: 0: 0: 0).

These 2 rows form rib.

Work in rib for 7 rows more, ending with WS facing for next row.

Row 10 (WS) Rib 4 (5: 6: 6: 7), M1, rib 4, M1, rib 12, M1, [rib 3, M1] twice, rib 12, M1, rib 4, M1, rib to end. 53 (55: 57: 57: 59) sts.

Change to size 8 (5mm) needles.

Starting and ending rows as indicated and repeating the 48 row patt repeat throughout, now work in patt from chart for Left Sleeve as foll:

**Inc 1 st at each end of 7th and every foll 8th row to 63 (65: 65: 75: 73) sts, then on every foll 10th row until there are 75 (77: 79: 81: 83) sts, taking inc sts into rev St st.

Work even until Sleeve measures 20¾ (20¾: 21¼: 21¼: 21½)in/53 (53: 54: 54: 55)cm from cast-on edge, ending with RS facing for next row.

Shape top of sleeve

Keeping patt correct, bind off 8 sts at beg of next 2 rows. 59 (61: 63: 65: 67) sts.

Dec 1 st at each end of next 3 rows, then on foll 3 alt rows, then on every foll 4th row until 43 (45: 47: 49: 51) sts rem.

Work 1 row.

Dec 1 st at each end of next and every foll alt row until 33 sts rem, then on foll 7 rows, ending with RS facing for next row. Bind off rem 19 sts.

RIGHT SLEEVE

Using size 6 (4mm) needles, cast on 46 (48: 50: 50: 52) sts.

Work in rib as given for Left Sleeve for 9 rows, ending with WS facing for next row.

Row 10 (WS) Inc in first st, rib 9 (10: 11: 11: 12), M1, rib 4, M1, rib 6, M1, rib 5, M1, rib 6, M1, rib 4, M1, rib to end. 53 (55: 57: 57: 59) sts.

Change to size 8 (5mm) needles.

Starting and ending rows as indicated and repeating the 24 row patt repeat throughout, now work in patt from chart for Right Sleeve as foll:

Complete as given for Left Sleeve from **.

FINISHING

Press lightly on WS following instructions on yarn label. Sew shoulder seams.

Right front band and collar

Using size 6 (4mm) needles, cast on 11 sts.

Row 1 (RS) K2, [P1, K1] 4 times, K1.

Row 2 K1, [P1, K1] 5 times.

These 2 rows form rib.

Work in rib until Band, when slightly stretched, fits up right front opening edge from cast-on edge to start of front slope shaping, sewing in place as you go along and ending with RS facing for next row.

Shape for collar

Inc 1 st at end (attached edge) of next and every foll alt row until there are 30 sts, taking inc sts into rib.

Work 1 row, ending at straight (unattached) edge.

Next row Bind off 14 sts in rib, then cast on 14 sts, rib to last st, inc in last st. 31 sts.

Cont in rib, inc 1 st at shaped edge of 2nd and foll 4 alt rows. 36 sts.

Work even until Collar section, unstretched, fits up right front slope and across to center back neck, sewing in place as you go along.

Bind off in rib.

Mark positions for 6 buttons on this band—first to come in row 5, last to come just below start of front slope shaping, and rem 4 buttons evenly spaced between.

Left front band and collar

Using size 6 (4mm) needles, cast on 11 sts.

Work in rib as given for Right Front Band and Collar for 4 rows, ending with RS facing for next row.

Row 5 (buttonhole row) (RS) Rib 4, bind off 2 sts (to make a buttonhole—cast on 2 sts over these bound-off sts on next row), rib to end.

Making 5 more buttonholes in this way to correspond

with positions marked for buttons on Right Front Band, work even until this Band, when slightly stretched, fits up left front opening edge from cast-on edge to start of front slope shaping, sewing in place as you go along and ending with RS facing for next row.

Shape for collar

Inc 1 st at beg (attached edge) of next and every foll alt row until there are 30 sts, ending at straight (unattached) edge and taking inc sts into rib.

Next row Bind off 14 sts in rib, then cast on 14 sts, rib to end.

Cont in rib, inc 1 st at shaped edge of next and foll 5 alt rows. 36 sts. Work even until Collar section, unstretched, fits up left front slope and across to center back neck, sewing in place as you go along. Bind off in rib.

Sew center back seam of collar sections.

Pocket tops (both alike)

Slip 30 sts from pocket holder onto size 6 (4mm) needles and rejoin yarn with RS facing.

Row 1 (RS) K15, M1, K15. 31 sts.
Row 2 P1, [K2, P1] 10 times.
Row 3 K1, [P2, K1] 10 times.
Rep rows 2 and 3 twice more, ending with WS facing for next row. Bind off in rib.

Sew pocket linings in place on inside, then neatly sew down ends of pocket tops. Sew side and sleeve seams. Sew sleeves into armholes. Sew on buttons.

ANCHOR GANSEY

Martin Storey

To fit chest					
40	42	44	46	48	in
102	107	112	117	122	cm

Finished measurements

AROUND CHEST

47½	49½	51	53	55	in
121	126	130	135	140	cm

LENGTH TO BACK NECK

26	26½	26¾	27	27½	in
66	67	68	69	70	cm

SLEEVE SEAM

20½	20½	21	21	21¼	in
52	52	53	53	54	cm

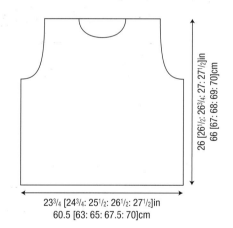

23¾ [24¾: 25½: 26½: 27½]in
60.5 [63: 65: 67.5: 70]cm

26 [26½: 26¾: 27: 27½]in
66 [67: 68: 69: 70]cm

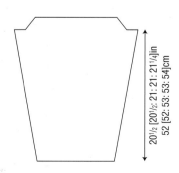

20½ [20½: 21: 21: 21¼]in
52 [52: 53: 53: 54]cm

YARNS

14 (15: 16: 17: 18) x 50g/1¾oz balls of Rowan *Pure Wool DK* in Mocha 017

NEEDLES

Pair of size 3 (3.25mm) knitting needles
Pair of size 6 (4mm) knitting needles
Size 3 (3.25mm) circular knitting needle
Cable needle

GAUGE

25 sts and 30 rows to 4in/10cm measured over patt using size 6 (4mm) needles *or size to obtain correct gauge.*

ABBREVIATIONS

See page 133.

SPECIAL ABBREVIATIONS

Tw2R = K2tog leaving sts on left needle, K first of these 2 sts again and slip both sts off left needle at same time;
Tw2L = K into back of second st of left needle, then K first st and slip both sts off left needle at same time;
C7B = slip next 4 sts onto cable needle and leave at back of work, K1 tbl, P1, K1 tbl, then [P1, K1 tbl] twice from cable needle.

BACK

Using size 3 (3.25mm) needles, cast on 151 (157: 163: 169: 175) sts.
Row 1 (RS) Knit.
Row 2 P2, *K2, P4; rep from * to last 5 sts, K2, P3.
Row 3 K2, *Tw2L, K4; rep from * to last 5 sts, Tw2L, K3.
Row 4 P2, *K1, P1, K1, P3; rep from * to last 5 sts, K1, P1, K1, P2.
Row 5 K3, *Tw2L, K4; rep from * to last 4 sts, Tw2L, K2.
Row 6 P3, *K2, P4; rep from * to last 4 sts, K2, P2.

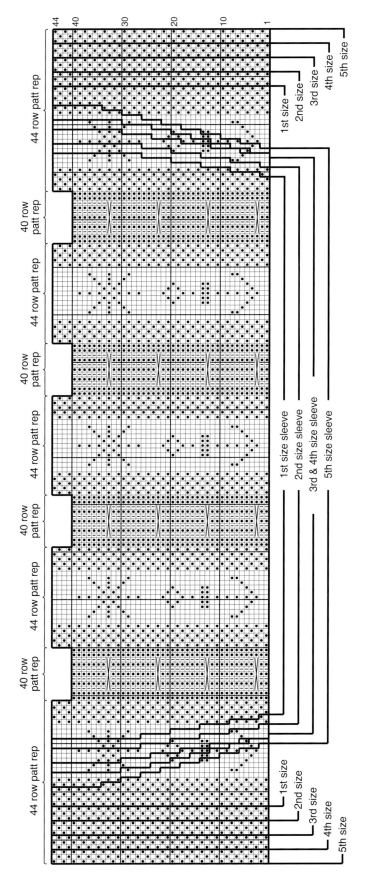

Row 7 Knit.

Row 8 Rep row 6.

Row 9 K3, *Tw2R, K4; rep from * to last 4 sts, Tw2R, K2.

Row 10 Rep row 4.

Row 11 K2, *Tw2R, K4; rep from * to last 5 sts, Tw2R, K3.

Row 12 Rep row 2.

These 12 rows form fancy rib.

Work in fancy rib for 21 rows more, ending with WS facing for next row.

Row 34 (WS) P7 (2: 5: 1: 4), P2tog, [P7 (8: 8: 9: 9), P2tog] 15 times, P to end. 135 (141: 147: 153: 159) sts.

Change to size 6 (4mm) needles.

Starting with a K row, work in St st until Back measures 6½in/17cm, ending with WS facing for next row.

Next row (WS) P8 (3: 6: 2: 5), M1, [P8 (9: 9: 10: 10), M1] 15 times, P to end. 151 (157: 163: 169: 175) sts.

Starting and ending rows as indicated and repeating the 40 and 44 row patt repeats throughout, work in patt from chart until Back measures 16½in/42cm from cast-on edge, ending with RS facing for next row.

Shape armholes

Keeping patt correct, bind off 6 sts at beg of next 2 rows. 139 (145: 151: 157: 163) sts.

Dec 1 st at each end of next and foll 5 alt rows. 127 (133: 139: 145: 151) sts.

Work even until armhole measures 9½ (9¾: 10¼: 10½: 11)in/24 (25: 26: 27: 28)cm, ending with RS facing for next row.

Shape back neck and shoulders

Next row (RS) Patt 40 (43: 45: 47: 49) sts and turn, leaving rem sts on a holder.

Work each side of neck separately.

Next row (WS) P2tog, patt 19 (19: 18: 17: 16) sts, [P2tog] 4 times, patt to end.

Break off yarn and leave rem 35 (38: 40: 42: 44) sts on a holder.

With RS facing, rejoin yarn to rem sts, bind off center 47 (47: 49: 51: 53) sts, patt to end.

Key
☐ K on RS, P on WS
▣ P on RS, K on WS
⊟ K1 tbl on RS, P1 tbl on WS
✕ C7B

Next row (WS) Patt 11 (14: 17: 20: 23) sts, [P2tog] 4 times, patt to last 2 sts, P2tog.

Break off yarn and leave rem 35 (38: 40: 42: 44) sts on another holder.

FRONT

Work as given for Back until 16 (18: 18: 18: 20) rows less have been worked than on Back to sts left on shoulder holders, ending with RS facing for next row.

Shape neck

Next row (RS) Patt 46 (50: 52: 54: 57) sts and turn, leaving rem sts on a holder.

Work each side of neck separately.

Keeping patt correct, dec 1 st at neck edge of next 4 rows, then on foll 2 (3: 3: 3: 4) alt rows, then on foll 4th row. 39 (42: 44: 46: 48) sts.

Work 2 rows, ending with WS facing for next row.

Next row (WS) Patt 20 (20: 19: 18: 17) sts, [P2tog] 4 times, patt to end. 35 (38: 40: 42: 44) sts.

Join shoulder seam

Holding WS of Front against WS of Back, bind off sts of left front shoulder seam with corresponding sts of left back shoulder seam (by taking one st of Front with corresponding st of Back).

With RS facing, rejoin yarn to rem sts, bind off center 35 (33: 35: 37: 37) sts, patt to end.

Keeping patt correct, dec 1 st at neck edge of next 4 rows, then on foll 2 (3: 3: 3: 4) alt rows, then on foll 4th row. 39 (42: 44: 46: 48) sts.

Work 2 rows, ending with WS facing for next row.

Next row (WS) Patt 11 (14: 17: 20: 23) sts, [P2tog] 4 times, patt to end. 35 (38: 40: 42: 44) sts.

Join shoulder seam

Holding WS of Front against WS of Back, bind off sts of right front shoulder seam with corresponding sts of right back shoulder seam (by taking one st of Front with corresponding st of Back).

SLEEVES

Using size 3 (3.25mm) needles, cast on 67 (67: 67: 73: 73) sts.

Work in fancy rib as given for Back for 33 rows, ending with WS facing for next row.

Row 34 (WS) P1 (4: 5: 2: 4), P2tog, [P5 (6: 9: 4: 5), P2tog] 9 (7: 5: 11: 9) times, P to end. 57 (59: 61: 61: 63) sts.

Change to size 6 (4mm) needles.

Starting with a K row, work in St st, shaping sides by inc 1 st at each end of 3rd and every foll 4th (4th: 4th: 4th: alt) row until there are 87 (95: 103: 103: 67) sts.

1ST, 2ND, AND 5TH SIZES ONLY

Inc 1 st at each end of every foll 6th (6th: -: -: 4th) row until there are 95 (99: -: -: 107) sts.

ALL SIZES

Work 2 (2: 2: 2: 0) rows, ending with WS facing for next row.

Next row (WS) P5 (7: 9: 9: 2), M1, [P5 (5: 5: 5: 6), M1] 17 times, P to end. 113 (117: 121: 121: 125) sts.

Starting and ending rows as indicated, work in patt from chart, inc 1 st at each end of 3rd (3rd: next: next: 3rd) and every foll 6th (6th: 6th: 4th: 4th) row until there are 123 (127: 133: 135: 143) sts, taking inc sts into patt.

4TH SIZE ONLY

Inc 1 st at each end of foll 6th row. 137 sts.

ALL SIZES

Work even until Sleeve measures 20½ (20½: 21: 21: 21¼)in/52 (52: 53: 53: 54)cm from cast-on edge, ending with RS facing for next row.

Shape top of sleeve

Keeping patt correct, bind off 6 sts at beg of next 2 rows. 111 (115: 121: 125: 131) sts.

Dec 1 st at each end of next and foll 5 alt rows, then on foll row, ending with RS facing for next row.

Bind off rem 97 (101: 107: 111: 117) sts.

FINISHING

Press lightly on WS following instructions on yarn label.

Neckband

With RS facing and using size 3 (3.25mm) circular needle, starting and ending at left shoulder seam, pick up and knit 18 (19: 19: 21: 22) sts down left side of neck, 30 (28: 30: 32: 32) sts from front, 18 (19: 19: 21: 22) sts up right side of neck, then 46 (46: 48: 50: 52) sts from back. 112 (112: 116: 124: 128) sts.

Round 1 (RS) *K2, P2; rep from * to end.

Rep this round until Neckband measures 2in/5cm.

Bind off in rib.

Sew side and sleeve seams. Sew sleeves into armholes.

RIBBED CARDIGAN

Wendy Baker

To fit chest					
40	42	44	46	48	in
102	107	112	117	122	cm

Finished measurements

AROUND CHEST					
46¾	48¾	50¾	52¾	54¾	in
119	124	129	134	139	cm

LENGTH TO BACK NECK					
26	26½	26¾	27	27½	in
66	67	68	69	70	cm

SLEEVE SEAM					
19½	19½	20	20	20½	in
50	50	51	51	52	cm

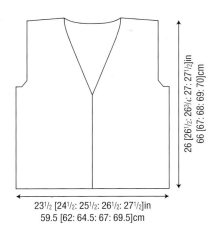

26 [26½: 26¾: 27: 27½]in
66 [67: 68: 69: 70]cm

23½ [24½: 25½: 26½: 27½]in
59.5 [62: 64.5: 67: 69.5]cm

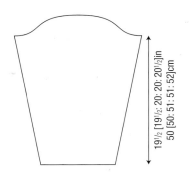

19½ [19½: 20: 20: 20½]in
50 [50: 51: 51: 52]cm

YARNS

Rowan *RYC Cashsoft DK*:

MC Thunder 518   12 (12: 13: 13: 14) x 50g/1¾oz balls
A Lichen 523   3 (3: 3: 4: 4) x 50g/1¾oz balls
B Black 519   1 (1: 1: 1: 1) x 50g/1¾oz balls

NEEDLES

Pair of size 3 (3.25mm) knitting needles
Pair of size 6 (4mm) knitting needles

EXTRAS

5 buttons

GAUGE

24 sts and 30 rows to 4in/10cm measured over patt using size 6 (4mm) needles *or size to obtain correct gauge.*

ABBREVIATIONS

See page 133.

BACK

Using size 3 (3.25mm) needles and A, cast on 143 (149: 155: 161: 167) sts.
Row 1 (RS) K1, *P1, K1; rep from * to end.
Row 2 P1, *K1, P1; rep from * to end.
These 2 rows form rib.
Work in rib for 14 rows more, ending with RS facing for next row.
Break off A and join in B.
Change to size 6 (4mm) needles.
Work in patt as foll:
Row 1 (RS) K3 (6: 0: 3: 6), P2, *K7, P2; rep from * to last 3 (6: 0: 3: 6) sts, K3 (6: 0: 3: 6).
Row 2 P3 (6: 0: 3: 6), K2, *P7, K2; rep from * to last 3 (6: 0: 3: 6) sts, P3 (6: 0: 3: 6).
These 2 rows form patt.

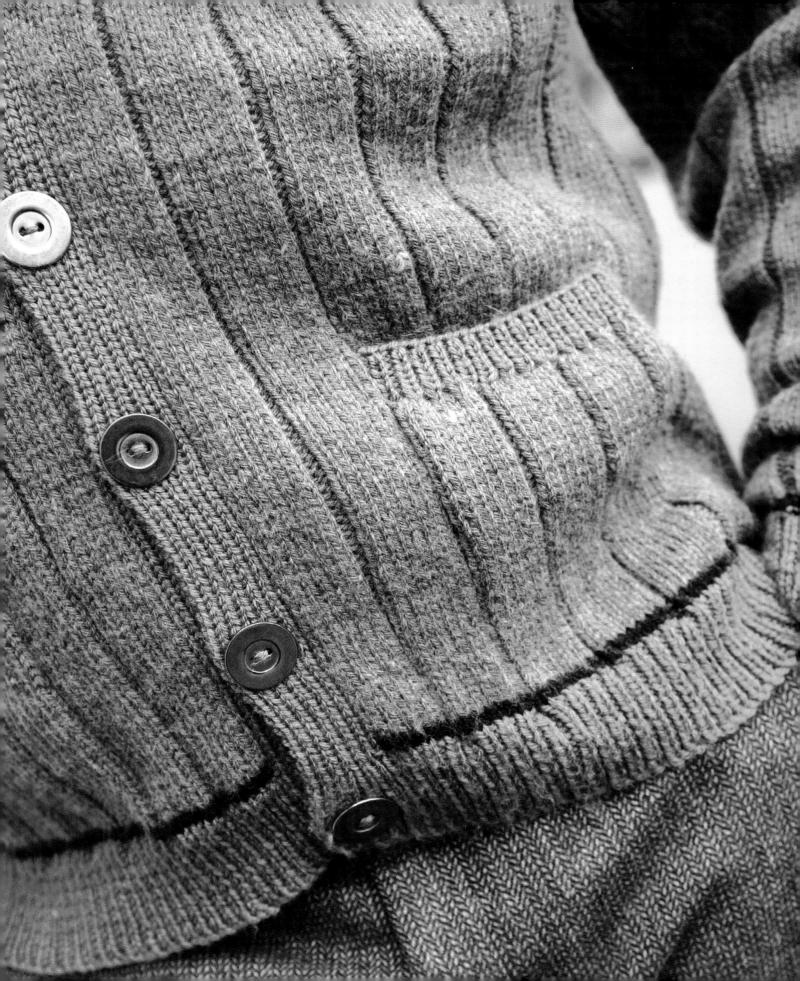

Break off B and join in MC.

Work even in patt until Back measures 15¾in/40cm, ending with RS facing for next row.

Shape armholes

Keeping patt correct, bind off 8 sts at beg of next 2 rows. 127 (133: 139: 145: 151) sts.

Dec 1 st at each end of next and foll 5 alt rows. 115 (121: 127: 133: 139) sts.

Work even until armhole measures 9½ (9¾: 10¼: 10½: 11)in/24 (25: 26: 27: 28)cm, ending with RS facing for next row.

Shape back neck

Next row (RS) Patt 35 (38: 40: 42: 44) sts and turn, leaving rem sts on a holder.

Work each side of neck separately.

Keeping patt correct, dec 1 st at neck edge of next 4 rows. 31 (34: 36: 38: 40) sts.

Work 1 row, ending with RS facing for next row.

Shape shoulder

Bind off 10 (11: 12: 13: 13) sts at beg of next and foll alt row.

Work 1 row.

Bind off rem 11 (12: 12: 12: 14) sts.

With RS facing, rejoin yarn to rem sts, bind off center 45 (45: 47: 49: 51) sts dec 5 sts evenly across, patt to end.

Complete to match first side, reversing shapings.

POCKET LININGS (make 2)

Using size 6 (4mm) needles and MC, cast on 28 sts.

Starting with a K row, work in St st for 37 rows, ending with WS facing for next row.

Row 38 (WS) P5, [M1, P6] 3 times, M1, P5. 32 sts.

Break off yarn and leave sts on a holder.

LEFT FRONT

Using size 3 (3.25mm) needles and A, cast on 76 (80: 82: 86: 88) sts.

Row 1 (RS) *K1, P1; rep from * to last 2 sts, K2.

Row 2 *K1, P1; rep from * to end.

These 2 rows form rib.

Work in rib for 4 rows more, ending with RS facing for next row.

Row 7 (RS) Rib to last 8 sts, bind off 2 sts (to make first buttonhole—cast on 2 sts over these bound-off sts on next row), rib to end.

Work in rib for 8 rows more, ending with WS facing for next row.

Row 16 (WS) Rib 12 and slip these sts onto a holder, M1, rib to last 1 (0: 1: 0: 1) st, [inc in last st] 1 (0: 1: 0: 1) times. 66 (69: 72: 75: 78) sts.

Break off A and join in B.

Change to size 6 (4mm) needles.

Work in patt as foll:

Row 1 (RS) K3 (6: 0: 3: 6), *P2, K7; rep from * to end.

Row 2 *P7, K2; rep from * to last 3 (6: 0: 3: 6) sts, P3 (6: 0: 3: 6).

These 2 rows form patt.

Break off B and join in MC.

Work even in patt for 36 rows more, ending with RS facing for next row.

Place pocket

Next row (RS) Patt 17 (18: 19: 20: 21) sts, slip next 32 sts onto a holder and, in their place, patt across 32 sts of first Pocket Lining, patt to end.

Cont in patt until 12 rows less have been worked than on Back to start of armhole shaping, ending with RS facing for next row.

Shape front slope

Next row (RS) Patt to last 3 sts, K2tog, K1.

Working all front slope decreases as set by last row, dec 1 st at front slope edge of 4th and foll 4th row. 63 (66: 69: 72: 75) sts.

Work 3 rows, ending with RS facing for next row.

Shape armhole

Keeping patt correct, bind off 8 sts at beg and dec 1 st at end of next row. 54 (57: 60: 63: 66) sts.

Work 1 row.

Dec 1 st at armhole edge of next and foll 5 alt rows **and at the same time** dec 1 st at front slope edge of 3rd and every foll 4th row. 45 (48: 51: 54: 57) sts.

Dec 1 st at front slope edge **only** on 4th and 13 (11: 13: 14: 16) foll 4th rows, then on 0 (2: 1: 1: 0) foll 6th rows. 31 (34: 36: 38: 40) sts.

Work even until Left Front matches Back to start of shoulder shaping, ending with RS facing for next row.

Shape shoulder

Bind off 10 (11: 12: 13: 13) sts at beg of next and foll alt row.

Work 1 row.

Bind off rem 11 (12: 12: 12: 14) sts.

RIGHT FRONT

Using size 3 (3.25mm) needles and A, cast on 76 (80: 82: 86: 88) sts.

Row 1 (RS) K2, *P1, K1; rep from * to end.

Row 2 *P1, K1; rep from * to end.

These 2 rows form rib.

Work in rib for 13 rows more, ending with WS facing for next row.

Row 16 (WS) [Inc in first st] 1 (0: 1: 0: 1) times, rib to last 12 sts, M1 and turn, leaving last 12 sts on a holder. 66 (69: 72: 75: 78) sts.

Break off A and join in B.

Change to size 6 (4mm) needles.

Work in patt as foll:

Row 1 (RS) *K7, P2; rep from * to last 3 (6: 0: 3: 6) sts, K3 (6: 0: 3: 6).

Row 2 P3 (6: 0: 3: 6), *K2, P7; rep from * to end.

These 2 rows form patt.

Break off B and join in MC.

Work even in patt for 36 rows more, ending with RS facing for next row.

Place pocket

Next row (RS) Patt 17 (19: 21: 23: 25) sts, slip next 32 sts onto a holder and, in their place, patt across 32 sts of second Pocket Lining, patt to end.

Cont in patt until 12 rows less have been worked than on Back to start of armhole shaping, ending with RS facing for next row.

Shape front slope

Next row (RS) K1, sl 1, K1, psso, patt to end.

Working all front slope decreases as set by last row, complete to match Left Front, reversing shapings.

SLEEVES

Using size 3 (3.25mm) needles and A, cast on 79 (81: 83: 83: 85) sts.

Work in rib as given for Back for 16 rows, ending with RS facing for next row.

Break off A and join in B.

Change to size 6 (4mm) needles.

Work in patt as foll:

Row 1 (RS) P0 (1: 0: 0: 0), K7 (7: 0: 0: 1), *P2, K7; rep from * to last 0 (1: 2: 2: 3) sts, P0 (1: 2: 2: 2), K0 (0: 0: 0: 1).

Row 2 K0 (1: 0: 0: 0), P7 (7: 0: 0: 1), *K2, P7; rep from * to last 0 (1: 2: 2: 3) sts, K0 (1: 2: 2: 2), P0 (0: 0: 0: 1).

These 2 rows form patt.

Break off B and join in MC.

Work in patt, shaping sides by inc 1 st at each end of 3rd (next: next: next: next) and every foll 6th (4th: 4th: 4th: 4th) row until there are 119 (87: 91: 103: 109) sts, taking inc sts into patt.

2ND, 3RD, 4TH, AND 5TH SIZES ONLY

Inc 1 st at each end of every foll 6th row until there are (123: 127: 131: 135) sts.

ALL SIZES

Work even until Sleeve measures 19½ (19½: 20: 20: 20½)in/50 (50: 51: 51: 52)cm from cast-on edge, ending with RS facing for next row.

Shape top of sleeve

Keeping patt correct, bind off 8 sts at beg of next 2 rows. 103 (107: 111: 115: 119) sts.

Dec 1 st at each end of 3rd and 2 foll 4th rows. 97 (101: 105: 109: 113) sts.

Work 1 row.

Bind off 6 sts at beg of next 10 rows, ending with RS facing for next row.

Bind off rem 37 (41: 45: 49: 53) sts.

FINISHING

Press lightly on WS following instructions on yarn label. Sew shoulder seams.

Right front band

Slip 12 sts from right front holder onto size 3 (3.25mm) needles and rejoin A with WS facing.

Work in rib as set until Band, when slightly stretched, fits up right front opening edge from cast-on edge to start of front slope shaping, up right front slope, and across to center back neck, sewing in place as you go along and ending with RS facing for next row.

Bind off in rib.

Mark positions for 5 buttons on this band—first to come level with buttonhole already worked in left front, last to come just below start of front slope shaping, and rem 3 buttons evenly spaced between.

Left front band

Slip 12 sts from left front holder onto size 3 (3.25mm) needles and rejoin A with RS facing.

Work in rib as set until Band, when slightly stretched, fits up left front opening edge from cast-on edge to start of front slope shaping, up right front slope, and across to center back neck, sewing in place as you go along,

ending with RS facing for next row and making 4 buttonholes more to correspond with positions marked for buttons as foll:

Buttonhole row (RS) Rib 4, bind off 2 sts (to make a buttonhole—cast on 2 sts over these bound-off sts on next row), rib to end.

When band is complete, bind off in rib.

Sew center back seam of bands.

Pocket tops (both alike)

Slip 32 sts from pocket holder onto size 3 (3.25mm) needles and rejoin A with RS facing.

Row 1 (RS) K2tog, *P1, K1; rep from * to end. 31 sts.

Starting with row 2, work in rib as given for Back for 3 rows, ending with RS facing for next row.

Bind off in rib.

Sew pocket linings in place on inside, then neatly sew down ends of pocket tops. Sew side and sleeve seams. Sew sleeves into armholes. Sew on buttons.

BIRD'S-EYE MITTENS
Martin Storey

SIZE
The finished mittens measure 8½in/22cm around hand.

YARNS
1 x 50g/1¾oz balls of Rowan *Felted Tweed* in each of **MC** (Midnight 133) and **A** (Wheat 156)

NEEDLES
Pair of size 2 (3mm) knitting needles
Pair of size 5 (3.75mm) knitting needles

GAUGE
23 sts and 32 rows to 4in/10cm measured over St st using size 5 (3.75mm) needles *or size to obtain correct gauge.*

ABBREVIATIONS
See page 133.

RIGHT MITTEN
Using size 3 (3mm) needles and MC, cast on 50 sts.
Row 1 (RS) K2, *P2, K2; rep from * to end.
Row 2 P2, *K2, P2; rep from * to end.
These 2 rows form rib.
Work in rib for 16 rows more, ending with RS facing for next row.
Change to size 5 (3.75mm) needles.
Join in A.
Stranding yarn not in use loosely across WS of work, work in patt as foll:
Row 1 (RS) Using MC knit.
Row 2 Using MC purl.
Row 3 Using MC K2, *using A K1, using MC K1; rep from * to end.
Row 4 Rep row 2.
Row 5 Rep row 1.
Row 6 *Using MC P1, using A P1; rep from * to last

2 sts, using MC P2.

These 6 rows form patt.

Shape thumb gusset

Next row (RS) Patt 26 sts, place marker on right needle, M1, patt 1 st, M1, place 2nd marker on right needle, patt to end. 52 sts.

Work 3 rows.

Next row Patt to first marker, slip marker onto right needle, M1, patt to 2nd marker, M1, slip 2nd marker onto right needle, patt to end.

Rep last 4 rows 3 times more. 60 sts.

Work 1 row, ending with RS facing for next row.

Next row (RS) Patt 38 sts and turn.

Next row Cast on and P 5 sts, P13 and turn.

**Work 11 rows more on these 18 sts only for thumb, ending with WS facing for next row.

Break off A and cont using MC only.

Starting with row 2, work in rib for 3 rows, ending with RS facing for next row.

Bind off in rib.

Sew thumb seam.

With RS facing, pick up and knit 3 sts from base of thumb, K to end. 50 sts.

Work in patt for 13 rows more, ending with RS facing for next row.

Break off A and complete using MC only.

Starting with row 1, work in rib for 4 rows, ending with RS facing for next row.

Bind off in rib.

LEFT MITTEN

Work as given for Right Mitten to start of thumb gusset shaping.

Shape thumb gusset

Next row (RS) Patt 23 sts, place marker on right needle, M1, patt 1 st, M1, place 2nd marker on right needle, patt to end. 52 sts.

Work 3 rows.

Next row Patt to first marker, slip marker onto right needle, M1, patt to 2nd marker, M1, slip 2nd marker onto right needle, patt to end.

Rep last 4 rows 3 times more. 60 sts.

Work 1 row, ending with RS facing for next row.

Next row (RS) Patt 35 sts and turn.

Next row Cast on and P 5 sts, P13 and turn.

Complete as given for Right Mitten from **.

FINISHING

Press lightly on WS following instructions on yarn label.

Sew side seam.

BIRD'S EYE JACKET

Martin Storey

To fit chest

40	42	44	46	48	in
102	107	112	117	122	cm

Finished measurements

AROUND CHEST

48¾	50¾	52¾	54¾	56½	in
124	129	134	139	144	cm

LENGTH TO BACK NECK

26	26½	26¾	27	27½	in
66	67	68	69	70	cm

SLEEVE SEAM

20¾	20½	20¾	20¾	21¼	in
52	52	53	53	54	cm

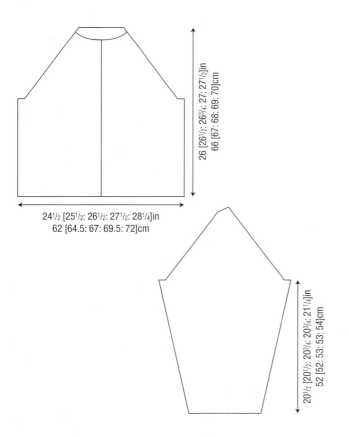

26 [26½: 26¾: 27: 27½]in
66 [67: 68: 69: 70]cm

24½ [25½: 26½: 27½: 28¼]in
62 [64.5: 67: 69.5: 72]cm

20½ [20½: 20¾: 20¾: 21¼]in
52 [52: 53: 53: 54]cm

YARNS

8 (9: 9: 10: 10) x 100g/3½oz balls of Rowan *Scottish Tweed Chunky* in **MC** (Winter Navy 021) and 2 (2: 3: 4: 4) balls in **A** (Lewis Blue 032)

NEEDLES

Pair of size 6 (4mm) knitting needles
Pair of size 8 (5mm) knitting needles

EXTRAS

6 buttons

GAUGE

16 sts and 20 rows to 4in/10cm measured over patt using size 8 (5mm) needles *or size to obtain correct gauge.*

ABBREVIATIONS

See page 133.

SPECIAL NOTE

When working patt from chart, strand yarn not in use loosely across WS of work. Work odd-numbered rows as RS (K) rows, reading them from right to left, and even-numbered rows as WS (P) rows, reading them from left to right.

BACK

Using size 6 (4mm) needles and MC, cast on 98 (102: 106: 110: 114) sts.
Row 1 (RS) Using MC, K2, *P2, K2; rep from * to end.
Row 2 Using MC, P2, *K2, P2; rep from * to end.
These 2 rows form rib.
Join in A.
Row 3 Using A, knit.
Row 4 Using A, P2, *K2, P2; rep from * to end.
Row 5 Using MC, knit.

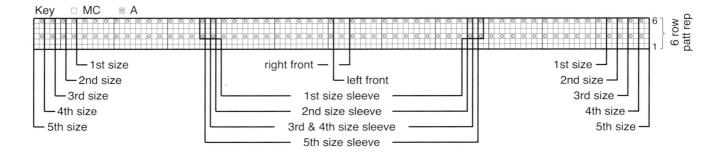

Key □ MC ◉ A

1st size
2nd size
3rd size
4th size
5th size

right front
left front
1st size sleeve
2nd size sleeve
3rd & 4th size sleeve
5th size sleeve

1st size
2nd size
3rd size
4th size
5th size

6
1

6 row patt rep

Row 6 Rep row 2.

Rows 7 to 10 Rep rows 3 to 6.

Rows 11 to 20 Rep rows 1 and 2 five times, inc 1 st at end of last row and ending with RS facing for next row. 99 (103: 107: 111: 115) sts.

Change to size 8 (5mm) needles.

Starting and ending rows as indicated and repeating the 6 row patt repeat throughout, now work in patt from chart as foll:

Work even in patt until Back measures 15in/38cm from cast-on edge, ending with RS facing for next row.

Shape raglan armholes

Keeping patt correct, bind off 5 sts at beg of next 2 rows. 89 (93: 97: 101: 105) sts.

Next row (RS) Using MC K1, sl 1, K1, psso, patt to last 3 sts, using MC K2tog, K1.

Next row Using MC P1, P2tog, patt to last 3 sts, using MC P2tog tbl, P1.

Working all raglan armhole decreases as set by last 2 rows, dec 1 st at each end of next 11 (13: 13: 13: 13) rows, then on every foll alt row until 23 (23: 25: 27: 29) sts rem.

Work 1 row, ending with RS facing for next row.

Bind off.

LEFT FRONT

Using size 6 (4mm) needles and MC, cast on 50 (54: 54: 58: 58) sts.

Work rows 1 to 20 as given for Back but inc (dec: inc: dec: inc) 1 st at end of last row and ending with RS facing for next row. 51 (53: 55: 57: 59) sts.

Change to size 8 (5mm) needles.

Starting and ending rows as indicated, now work in patt from chart as foll:

Work 6 rows, ending with RS facing for next row.

Place pocket

Next row (RS) Patt 15 sts and turn, leaving rem 36 (38:

40: 42: 44) sts on a holder.

Next row Using MC cast on and P 24 sts (for pocket lining), patt to end. 39 sts.

Working 24 pocket lining sts in St st using MC and rem 15 side front sts in patt, work 26 rows on these 39 sts, ending with RS facing for next row.

Next row (RS) Patt 15 sts and slip these sts onto another holder, bind off rem 24 sts.

Break off yarn.

With RS facing, rejoin yarns to 36 (38: 40: 42: 44) sts on first holder, patt to end.

Work in patt for 28 rows more on these sts for pocket front, ending with WS facing for next row.

Join sections

Next row (WS) Patt across 36 (38: 40: 42: 44) sts of pocket front, then patt across 15 sts of side front. 51 (53: 55: 57: 59) sts.

Work even until Left Front matches Back to start of raglan armhole shaping, ending with RS facing for next row.

Shape raglan armhole

Keeping patt correct, bind off 5 sts at beg of next row. 46 (48: 50: 52: 54) sts.

Work 1 row.

Working all raglan armhole decreases in same way as given for Back, dec 1 st at raglan armhole edge of next 13 (15: 15: 15: 15) rows, then on every foll alt row until 20 (21: 22: 23: 25) sts rem, ending with WS facing for next row.

Shape neck

Keeping patt correct, bind off 7 (6: 7: 8: 8) sts at beg of next row. 13 (15: 15: 15: 17) sts.

Dec 1 st at neck edge of next 3 rows, then on foll 3 (4: 4: 4: 5) alt rows **and at the same time** dec 1 st at raglan armhole edge of next and every foll alt row. 2 sts.

Work 1 row, ending with RS facing for next row.

Next row (RS) K2tog and fasten off.

RIGHT FRONT

Using size 6 (4mm) needles and MC, cast on 50 (54: 54: 58: 58) sts.

Work rows 1 to 20 as given for Back but inc (dec: inc: dec: inc) 1 st at beg of last row and ending with RS facing for next row. 51 (53: 55: 57: 59) sts.

Change to size 8 (5mm) needles.

Starting and ending rows as indicated, now work in patt from chart as foll:

Work 6 rows, ending with RS facing for next row.

Place pocket

Next row (RS) Patt 36 (38: 40: 42: 44) sts and turn, leaving rem 15 sts on a holder.

Work in patt for 28 rows more on these sts for pocket front, ending with WS facing for next row.

Break off yarn and leave these sts on another holder. With RS facing, rejoin yarns to 15 sts on first holder and work as foll:

Next row (RS) Using MC cast on and K 24 sts (for pocket lining), patt to end. 39 sts.

Working 24 pocket lining sts in St st using MC and rem 15 side front sts in patt, work 26 rows on these 39 sts, ending with RS facing for next row.

Next row (RS) Bind off 24 sts, patt to end. 15 sts.

Join sections

Next row (WS) Patt across 15 sts of side front, then patt across 36 (38: 40: 42: 44) sts of pocket front. 51 (53: 55: 57: 59) sts.

Complete to match Left Front, reversing shapings.

SLEEVES

Using size 6 (4mm) needles and MC, cast on 46 (46: 50: 50: 50) sts.

Work rows 1 to 20 as given for Back but dec (inc: dec: dec: inc) 1 st at end of last row and ending with RS facing for next row. 45 (47: 49: 49: 51) sts.

Change to size 8 (5mm) needles.

Starting and ending rows as indicated, now work in patt from chart as foll:

Inc 1 st at each end of 3rd and every foll 4th row until there are 69 (71: 71: 77: 77) sts, then on every foll 6th row until there are 79 (81: 83: 85: 87) sts, taking inc sts into patt.

Work even until Sleeve measures 20½ (20½: 20¾: 20¾: 21¼)in/52 (52: 53: 53: 54)cm from cast-on edge, ending with RS facing for next row.

Shape raglan

Keeping patt correct, bind off 5 sts at beg of next 2 rows. 69 (71: 73: 75: 77) sts.

Working all raglan decreases in same way as given for raglan armhole decreases, dec 1 st at each end of next 13 rows, then on every foll alt row until 7 sts rem.

Work 1 row, ending with RS facing for next row.

LEFT SLEEVE ONLY

Place marker at beg of last row to denote front neck point.

RIGHT SLEEVE ONLY

Place marker at end of last row to denote front neck point.

BOTH SLEEVES

Dec 1 st at marked front neck edge of next 3 rows **and at the same time** dec 1 st at back raglan edge of next and foll alt row. 2 sts.

Next row (WS) P2tog and fasten off.

FINISHING

Press lightly on WS following instructions on yarn label. Sew raglan seams.

Button band
Using size 6 (4mm) needles and MC, cast on 7 sts.
Work in garter st until Band, when slightly stretched, fits
up right front opening edge from cast-on edge to neck
shaping, sewing in place as you go along and ending
with RS facing for next row.
Bind off.
Mark positions for 6 buttons on this band—first to come
in row 7, last to come just below neck shaping, and rem
4 buttons evenly spaced between.

Buttonhole band
Using size 6 (4mm) needles and MC, cast on 7 sts.
Work in garter st until Band, when slightly stretched, fits
up left front opening edge from cast-on edge to neck
shaping, sewing in place as you go along, ending with
RS facing for next row and making 6 buttonholes to
correspond with positions marked for buttons as foll:
Buttonhole row (RS) K2, K2tog, yo (to make a
buttonhole), K3.
When band is complete, bind off.

Collar
Using size 6 (4mm) needles and MC, cast on 86 (90: 94:
98: 106) sts.
Work rows 1 to 10 as given for Back.
Break off A and cont using MC only.
Now rep rows 1 and 2 only until Collar measures
4¾in/12cm from cast-on edge, ending with RS facing for
next row.
Keeping rib correct, bind off 8 (8: 9: 9: 10) sts at beg of
next 8 rows.
Bind off rem 22 (26: 22: 26: 26) sts.
Positioning row-end edges of collar halfway across top
of front bands, sew shaped bound-off edge of collar to
neck edge.

Pocket borders (both alike)
With RS facing, using size 6 (4mm) needles and MC, pick
up and knit 25 sts evenly along row-end pocket opening
edge.
Work in garter st for 6 rows, ending with WS facing for
next row.
Bind off knitwise (on WS).
Sew pocket linings in place on inside, then neatly sew
down ends of pocket borders. Sew side and sleeve
seams. Sew on buttons.

ARGYLL V-NECK

Martin Storey

To fit chest					
40	42	44	46	48	in
102	107	112	117	122	cm
Finished measurements					
AROUND CHEST					
44	45½	48	50	52¼	in
112	116	122	127	133	cm
LENGTH TO BACK NECK					
24	24½	24¾	25	25½	in
61	62	63	64	65	cm

YARNS

Rowan *Scottish Tweed 4 ply*:

MC Celtic Mix 0226 6 (7: 8: 9: 9) x 25g/⅞oz balls

A Rust 0094 4 (4: 5: 5: 5) x 25g/⅞oz balls

B Apple 0153 4 (4: 5: 5: 5) x 25g/⅞oz balls

NEEDLES

Pair of size 2 (2.75mm) knitting needles

Pair of size 3 (3.25mm) knitting needles

Size 2 (2.75mm) circular knitting needle

GAUGE

26 sts and 38 rows to 4in/10cm measured over patterned St st using size 3 (3.25mm) needles *or size to obtain correct gauge.*

ABBREVIATIONS

See page 133.

SPECIAL NOTE

When working patt from chart, use a separate ball of yarn for each block of color, twisting yarns together on WS where they meet to avoid holes forming. Work odd-numbered rows as RS (K) rows, reading them from right to left, and even-numbered rows as WS (P) rows, reading them from left to right.

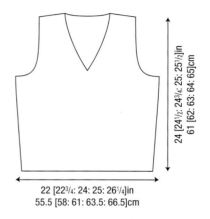

22 [22¾: 24: 25: 26¼]in
55.5 [58: 61: 63.5: 66.5]cm

24 [24½: 24¾: 25: 25½]in
61 [62: 63: 64: 65]cm

BACK

Using size 2 (2.75mm) needles and MC, cast on 134 (138: 146: 154: 162) sts.

Row 1 (RS) K2, *P2, K2; rep from * to end.

Row 2 P2, *K2, P2; rep from * to end.

These 2 rows form rib.

Work in rib for 28 rows more, dec (inc: inc: dec: dec) 1 st at end of last row and ending with RS facing for next row. 133 (139: 147: 153: 161) sts.

Change to size 3 (3.25mm) needles.

Starting and ending rows as indicated, joining in and breaking off colors as required and repeating the 46 row patt repeat throughout, now work in patt from chart as foll:

Inc 1 st at each end of 17th and every foll 16th row until there are 145 (151: 159: 165: 173) sts, taking inc sts into patt.

Work even until Back measures 14½in/37cm from cast-on edge, ending with RS facing for next row.

Shape armholes

Keeping patt correct, bind off 8 (9: 9: 10: 10) sts at beg of next 2 rows. 129 (133: 141: 145: 153) sts.**

Dec 1 st at each end of next 7 (7: 9: 9: 11) rows, then on

foll 5 (6: 6: 7: 7) alt rows, then on 4 foll 4th rows. 97 (99: 103: 105: 109) sts.

Work even until armhole measures 9½ (9¾: 10¼: 10½: 11)in/24 (25: 26: 27: 28)cm, ending with RS facing for next row.

Shape shoulders and back neck

Bind off 9 (10: 10: 10: 10) sts at beg of next 2 rows. 79 (79: 83: 85: 89) sts.

Next row (RS) Bind off 9 (10: 10: 10: 10) sts, patt until there are 14 (13: 14: 14: 15) sts on right needle and turn, leaving rem sts on a holder.

Work each side of neck separately.

Bind off 4 sts at beg of next row.

Bind off rem 10 (9: 10: 10: 11) sts.

With RS facing, rejoin yarns to rem sts, bind off center 33 (33: 35: 37: 39) sts, patt to end.

Complete to match first side, reversing shapings.

FRONT

Work as given for Back to **.

Dec 1 st at each end of next 7 (7: 9: 9: 11) rows, then on foll 4 (4: 3: 3: 2) alt rows. 107 (111: 117: 121: 127) sts.

Work 1 row, ending with RS facing for next row.

Divide for neck

Next row (RS) K2tog, patt 51 (53: 56: 58: 61) sts and turn, leaving rem sts on a holder.

Work each side of neck separately.

Keeping patt correct, dec 1 st at armhole edge of 4th (2nd: 2nd: 2nd: 2nd) and foll 0 (0: 1: 2: 3) alt rows, then on 3 (4: 4: 4: 4) foll 4th rows **and at the same time** dec 1 st at neck edge of 2nd and foll 7 (6: 7: 7: 7) alt rows, then on 0 (1: 1: 1: 2) foll 4th rows. 40 (41: 42: 43: 44) sts.

Dec 1 st at neck edge **only** on 2nd (4th: 4th: 2nd: 4th) and every foll 4th row until 28 (29: 30: 30: 31) sts rem.

Work even until Front matches Back to start of shoulder shaping, ending with RS facing for next row.

Shape shoulder

Bind off 9 (10: 10: 10: 10) sts at beg of next and foll alt row.

Work 1 row.

Bind off rem 10 (9: 10: 10: 11) sts.

With RS facing, slip center st onto a holder, rejoin yarns to rem sts, patt to last 2 sts, K2tog.

Complete to match first side, reversing shapings.

FINISHING

Press lightly on WS following instructions on yarn label.

Sew shoulder seams.

Neckband

With RS facing, using size 2 (2.75mm) circular needle and MC, starting and ending at left shoulder seam, pick up and knit 76 (80: 84: 88: 92) sts down left side of neck, K st on holder at base of V and mark this st with a colored thread, pick up and knit 76 (80: 84: 88: 92) sts up right side of neck, then 42 (42: 42: 42: 46: 46) sts from back. 195 (203: 211: 223: 231) sts.

Round 1 (RS) *K2, P2; rep from * to within 4 sts of marked st, K2, K2tog tbl, K marked st, K2tog, **K2, P2; rep from ** to end.

This round sets position of rib as given for Back.

Keeping rib correct as now set, cont as foll:

Round 2 Rib to within 2 sts of marked st, K2tog tbl, K marked st, K2tog, rib to end.

Rep last round 8 times more. 175 (183: 191: 203: 211) sts.

Bind off in rib, still decreasing either side of marked st as before.

Armhole borders (both alike)

With RS facing, using size 2 (2.75mm) needles and MC, pick up and knit 142 (150: 158: 166: 174) sts evenly all around armhole edge. Starting with row 2, work in rib as given for Back for 8 rows, ending with WS facing for next row.

Bind off in rib (on WS).

Sew side and armhole border seams.

REVERSE STRIPE SWEATER

Martin Storey

To fit chest

40	42	44	46	48	in
102	107	112	117	122	cm

Finished measurements

AROUND CHEST

48	50	52	54	56¼	in
122	127	132	137	143	cm

LENGTH TO BACK NECK

26	26½	26½	26¾	27	in
66	67	67	68	69	cm

SLEEVE SEAM

20	20	20½	20½	20¾	in
51	51	52	52	53	cm

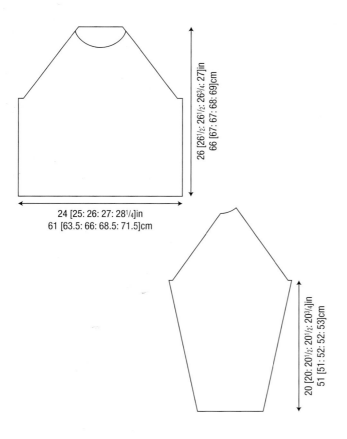

24 [25: 26: 27: 28¼]in
61 [63.5: 66: 68.5: 71.5]cm

26 [26½: 26½: 26¾: 27]in
66 [67: 67: 68: 69]cm

20 [20: 20½: 20½: 20¾]in
51 [51: 52: 52: 53]cm

YARNS

Rowan *Felted Tweed*:

MC Phantom 153   6 (7: 8: 8: 9) x 50g/1¾oz balls

A Dragon 147   3 (3: 4: 4: 5) x 50g/1¾oz balls

B Ginger 154   1 (2: 2: 3: 3) x 50g/1¾oz balls

NEEDLES

Pair of size 3 (3.25mm) knitting needles
Pair of size 5 (3.75mm) knitting needles
Size 3 (3.25mm) circular knitting needle

GAUGE

23 sts and 32 rows to 4in/10cm measured over rev St st using size 5 (3.75mm) needles *or size to obtain correct gauge.*

ABBREVIATIONS

See page 133.

BACK

Using size 3 (3.25mm) needles and MC, cast on 138 (146: 150: 158: 162) sts.

Row 1 (RS) K2, *P2, K2; rep from * to end.

Row 2 P2, *K2, P2; rep from * to end.

These 2 rows form rib.

Work in rib for 26 rows more, inc 1 (0: 1: 0: 1) st at each end of last row and ending with RS facing for next row. 140 (146: 152: 158: 164) sts.

Change to size 5 (3.75mm) needles.

Starting with a P row and joining in colors as required, work in striped rev St st as foll:

Rows 1 and 2 Using MC.

Rows 3 and 4 Using B.

Rows 5 and 6 Using MC.

Rows 7 and 8 Using A.

Rows 9 to 16 Rep rows 5 to 8 twice.

These 16 rows form striped rev St st.

Cont in striped rev St st until Back measures approximately 15in/38cm from cast-on edge, ending after stripe row 2 and with RS facing for next row.

Shape raglan armholes

Keeping stripes correct, bind off 5 sts at beg of next 2 rows. 130 (136: 142: 148: 154) sts.

Dec 1 st at each end of next 11 (15: 17: 19: 21) rows, then on every foll alt row until 32 (32: 34: 36: 38) sts rem.

Work 1 row, ending with RS facing for next row.

Bind off.

FRONT

Work as given for Back until 58 (60: 62: 64: 68) sts rem in raglan armhole shaping.

Work 1 row, ending with RS facing for next row.

Shape neck

Next row (RS) P2tog, P22 (24: 24: 24: 26) and turn, leaving rem sts on a holder.

Work each side of neck separately.

Keeping stripes correct, bind off 5 sts at beg of next row. 18 (20: 20: 20: 22) sts.

Dec 1 st at neck edge of 2nd and foll 3 rows, then on foll 1 (2: 2: 2: 3) alt rows, then on 2 foll 4th rows **and at the same time** dec 1 st at raglan armhole edge of next and foll 8 (9: 9: 9: 10) alt rows. 2 sts.

Work 1 row, ending with RS facing for next row.

Next row (RS) P2tog and fasten off.

With RS facing, rejoin yarns to rem sts, bind off center 10 (8: 10: 12: 12) sts, P to last 2 sts, P2tog.

Complete to match first side, reversing shapings.

SLEEVES

Using size 3 (3.25mm) needles and MC, cast on 58 (58: 62: 62: 62) sts.

Work in rib as given for Back for 28 rows, inc 0 (1: 0: 0: 1) st at each end of last row and ending with RS facing for next row. 58 (60: 62: 62: 64) sts.

Change to size 5 (3.75mm) needles.

Starting with a P row and stripe row 7 (7: 3: 3: 15), work in striped rev St st as given for Back, shaping sides by inc 1 st at each end of 3rd and every foll 4th row to 96 (98: 96: 102: 100) sts, then on every foll 6th row until there are 112 (114: 116: 118: 120) sts.

Work even until Sleeve measures approximately 20 (20: 20½: 20½: 20¾)in/51 (51: 52: 52: 53)cm from cast-on edge, ending after stripe row 2 and with RS facing for next row.

Shape raglan

Keeping stripes correct, bind off 5 sts at beg of next 2 rows. 102 (104: 106: 108: 110) sts.

Dec 1 st at each end of next 11 rows, then on every foll alt row until 10 sts rem.

Work 1 row, ending with RS facing for next row.

LEFT SLEEVE ONLY

Place marker at beg of last row to denote front neck point.

RIGHT SLEEVE ONLY

Place marker at end of last row to denote front neck point.

BOTH SLEEVES

Dec 1 st at marked front neck edge of next 5 rows **and at the same time** dec 1 st at back raglan armhole edge of next and 2 foll alt rows. 2 sts.

Work 1 row, ending with RS facing for next row.

Next row (RS) P2tog and fasten off.

FINISHING

Press lightly on WS following instructions on yarn label. Sew raglan seams.

Neckband

With RS facing, using size 3 (3.25mm) circular needle and MC, starting and ending at left back raglan seam, pick up and knit 9 sts from left sleeve, 23 (24: 24: 24: 27) sts down left side of neck, 10 (8: 10: 12: 12) sts from front, 23 (24: 24: 24: 27) sts up right side of neck, 9 sts from right sleeve, then 34 (34: 36: 38: 40) sts from back. 108 (108: 112: 116: 124) sts.

Round 1 (RS) *K2, P2; rep from * to end.

Rep this round 9 times more.

Bind off in rib.

Sew side and sleeve seams.

CABLE V-NECK

Martin Storey

To fit chest

40	42	44	46	48	in
102	107	112	117	122	cm

Finished measurements

AROUND CHEST

43	44¾	46½	48½	50¼	in
109	114	118	123	128	cm

LENGTH TO BACK NECK

24	24½	24¾	25	25½	in
61	62	63	64	65	cm

YARNS

9 (9: 10: 10: 11) x 50g/1¾oz balls of Rowan *RYC Baby Alpaca DK* in Zinc 204

NEEDLES

Pair of size 3 (3.25mm) knitting needles
Pair of size 6 (4mm) knitting needles
Size 3 (3.25mm) circular knitting needle

GAUGE

25 sts and 30 rows to 4in/10cm measured over patt using size 6 (4mm) needles *or size to obtain correct gauge.*

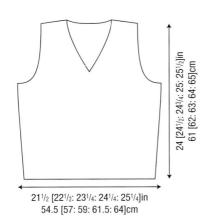

21½ [22½: 23¼: 24¼: 25¼]in
54.5 [57: 59: 61.5: 64]cm

24 [24½: 24¾: 25: 25½]in
61 [62: 63: 64: 65]cm

ABBREVIATIONS

See page 133.

SPECIAL ABBREVIATIONS

Cr3R = slip next st onto cable needle and leave at back of work, K2, then P1 from cable needle; **Cr3L** = slip next 2 sts onto cable needle and leave at front of work, P1, then K2 from cable needle; **C4B** = slip next 2 sts onto cable needle and leave at back of work, K2, then K2 from cable needle; **C4F** = slip next 2 sts onto cable needle and leave at front of work, K2, then K2 from cable needle; **C5B** = slip next 3 sts onto cable needle and leave at front of work, K2, slip center st from cable needle back onto left needle and P this st, then K2 from cable needle; **wrap 6** = K2, P2, K2 and slip these 6 sts onto cable needle, wrap yarn 4 times counterclockwise around these 6 sts then slip sts back onto right needle.

BACK

Using size 3 (3.25mm) needles, cast on 114 (120: 126: 132: 138) sts.

Row 1 (RS) P0 (1: 0: 0: 0), K0 (2: 2: 1: 0), *P2, K2; rep from * to last 2 (1: 0: 3: 2) sts, P2 (1: 0: 2: 2), K0 (0: 0: 1: 0).

Row 2 K0 (1: 0: 0: 0), P0 (2: 2: 1: 0), *K2, P2; rep from * to last 2 (1: 0: 3: 2) sts, K2 (1: 0: 2: 2), P0 (0: 0: 1: 0). These 2 rows form rib.

Work in rib for 17 rows more, ending with WS facing for next row.

Row 20 (WS) Rib 34 (37: 40: 43: 46), M1, [rib 1, M1] twice, rib 18, [M1, rib 1] 3 times, [rib 1, M1] 3 times, rib 18, M1, [rib 1, M1] twice, rib to end. 126 (132: 138: 144: 150) sts.

Change to size 6 (4mm) needles.

Starting and ending rows as indicated and repeating the 24 row patt repeat throughout, now work in patt from chart as foll:

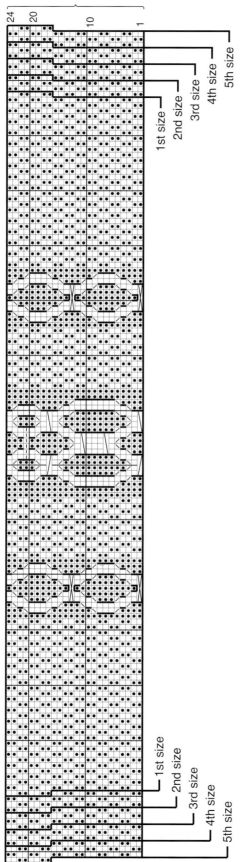

Inc 1 st at each end of 17th and every foll 16th row until there are 136 (142: 148: 154: 160) sts, taking inc sts into patt.

Work even until Back measures 14½in/37cm from cast-on edge, ending with RS facing for next row.

Shape armholes

Keeping patt correct, bind off 10 (11: 12: 13: 14) sts at beg of next 2 rows. 116 (120: 124: 128: 132) sts.**

Dec 1 st at each end of next 5 (5: 7: 7: 9) rows, then on foll 3 (4: 2: 3: 2) alt rows, then on 3 foll 4th rows. 94 (96: 100: 102: 104) sts.

Work even until armhole measures 9½ (9¾: 10¼: 10½: 11)in/24 (25: 26: 27: 28)cm, ending with RS facing for next row.

Shape shoulders and back neck

Bind off 9 (9: 10: 10: 10) sts at beg of next 2 rows. 76 (78: 80: 82: 84) sts.

Next row (RS) Bind off 9 (9: 10: 10: 10) sts, patt until there are 13 (14: 13: 13: 13) sts on right needle and turn, leaving rem sts on a holder.

Work each side of neck separately.

Bind off 4 sts at beg of next row.

Bind off rem 9 (10: 9: 9: 9) sts.

With RS facing, rejoin yarn to rem sts, bind off center 32 (32: 34: 36: 38) sts, patt to end.

Complete to match first side, reversing shapings.

FRONT

Work as given for Back to **.

Dec 1 st at each end of next 5 (5: 7: 7: 9) rows, then on foll 3 (4: 2: 3: 2) alt rows. 100 (102: 106: 108: 110) sts.

Work 3 (1: 3: 1: 1) rows, ending with RS facing for next row.

Divide for neck

Next row (RS) [Work 2 tog] 1 (0: 1: 0: 0) times, patt 47 (50: 50: 53: 54) sts and turn, leaving rem sts on a holder.

Work each side of neck separately.

Keeping patt correct, dec 1 st at armhole edge of 4th (2nd: 4th: 2nd: 2nd) and 1 (2: 1: 2: 2) foll 4th rows **and at the same time** dec 1 st at neck edge of 2nd and foll 3 (4: 3: 4: 4) alt rows. 42 (42: 45: 45: 46) sts.

Dec 1 st at neck edge **only** on 2nd and foll 10 (7: 9: 8: 9) foll alt rows, then on every foll 4th row until 27 (28: 29: 29: 29) sts rem.

Work even until Front matches Back to start of shoulder shaping, ending with RS facing for next row.

Shape shoulder

Bind off 9 (9: 10: 10: 10) sts at beg of next and foll
alt row.

Work 1 row.

Bind off rem 9 (10: 9: 9: 9) sts.

With RS facing, slip center 2 sts onto a holder, rejoin
yarn to rem sts, patt to last 2 (0: 2: 0: 0) sts, [work 2 tog]
1 (0: 1: 0: 0) times.

Complete to match first side, reversing shapings.

FINISHING

Press lightly on WS following instructions on yarn label.
Sew shoulder seams.

Neckband

With RS facing and using size 3 (3.25mm) circular
needle, starting and ending at left shoulder seam, pick
up and knit 60 (64: 68: 72: 76) sts down left side of neck,
K 2 sts from holder at base of V and place a marker
between these sts, pick up and knit 60 (64: 68: 72: 76)
sts up right side of neck, then 34 (34: 38: 38: 38) sts from
back. 156 (164: 176: 184: 192) sts.

Round 1 (RS) *K2, P2; rep from * to within 4 sts of
marker, K2, P1, K2tog, slip marker onto right needle, sl 1,
K1, psso, P1, **K2, P2; rep from ** to end.

This round sets position of rib as given for Back.

Keeping rib correct as now set, cont as foll:

Round 2 Rib to within 2 sts of marker, K2tog, slip marker
onto right needle, sl 1, K1, psso, rib to end.

Rep last round 6 times more. 140 (148: 160: 168:
176) sts.

Bind off in rib, still decreasing either side of marker
as before.

Armhole borders (both alike)

With RS facing and using size 3 (3.25mm) needles, pick
up and knit 130 (138: 146: 154: 162) sts evenly all around
armhole edge.

Next row (RS) *P2, K2; rep from * to last 2 sts, P2.

Next row *K2, P2; rep from * to last 2 sts, K2.

Rep last 2 rows twice more.

Bind off in rib (on WS).

Sew side and armhole border seams.

SHAWL COLLAR SWEATER

Martin Storey

To fit chest

40	42	44	46	48	in
102	107	112	117	122	cm

Finished measurements

AROUND CHEST

48½	51	52¼	55	56¼	in
123	130	133	140	143	cm

LENGTH TO BACK NECK

26	26½	26¾	27	27½	in
66	67	68	69	70	cm

SLEEVE SEAM

20½	20½	21	21	21¼	in
52	52	53	53	54	cm

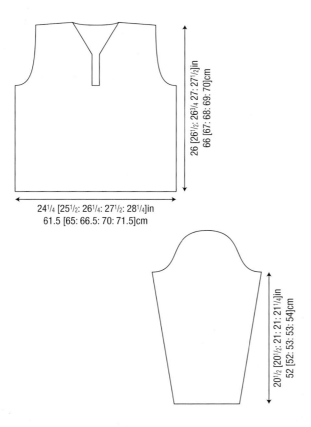

24¼ [25½: 26¼: 27½: 28¼]in
61.5 [65: 66.5: 70: 71.5]cm

26 [26½: 26¾ 27: 27½]in
66 [67: 68: 69: 70]cm

20½ [20½: 21: 21: 21¼]in
52 [52: 53: 53: 54]cm

YARNS

8 (9: 9: 10: 11) x 100g/3½oz balls of Rowan *Scottish Tweed Chunky* in **MC** (Lewis Grey 007) and 2 (2: 3: 3: 3) balls in **A** (Midnight 023)

NEEDLES

Pair of size 10½ (7mm) knitting needles
Pair of size 11 (8mm) knitting needles
Size 10½ (7mm) circular knitting needle

EXTRAS

1 toggle button

GAUGE

12 sts and 16 rows to 4in/10cm measured over St st using size 11 (8mm) needles *or size to obtain correct gauge.*

ABBREVIATIONS

See page 133.

BACK

Using size 10½ (7mm) needles and A, cast on 74 (78: 78: 82: 86) sts.

Row 1 (RS) K2, *P2, K2; rep from * to end.
Row 2 P2, *K2, P2; rep from * to end.
These 2 rows form rib.

Work in rib for 12 rows more, inc 0 (0: 1: 1: 0) st at each end of last row and ending with RS facing for next row. 74 (78: 80: 84: 86) sts.

Break off A and join in MC.

Change to size 11 (8mm) needles.

Starting with a K row, work in St st until Back measures 16½in/42cm from cast-on edge, ending with RS facing for next row.

Shape armholes

Bind off 4 sts at beg of next 2 rows. 66 (70: 72: 76: 78) sts.**

Dec 1 st at each end of next 3 rows, then on foll 2 (3: 3: 4: 4) alt rows, then on foll 4th row. 54 (56: 58: 60: 62) sts. Work even until armhole measures 9½ (9¾: 10¼: 10½: 11)in/24 (25: 26: 27: 28)cm, ending with RS facing for next row.

Shape shoulders and back neck

Next row (RS) Bind off 8 (8: 8: 9: 9) sts, K until there are 12 (13: 13: 13: 13) sts on right needle and turn, leaving rem sts on a holder.

Work each side of neck separately.

Bind off 4 sts at beg of next row.

Bind off rem 8 (9: 9: 9: 9) sts.

With RS facing, rejoin yarn to rem sts, bind off center 14 (14: 16: 16: 18) sts, K to end.

Complete to match first side, reversing shapings.

FRONT

Work as given for Back to **.

Dec 1 st at each end of next 3 rows, then on foll 1 (1: 2: 3: 2) alt rows. 58 (62: 62: 64: 68) sts.

Work 1 row, ending with RS facing for next row.

Divide for front opening

Next row (RS) K2tog, K25 (27: 27: 28: 30) and turn, leaving rem sts on a holder.

Work each side of neck separately.

Dec 1 st at armhole edge of 4th (2nd: 4th: 4th: 2nd) and foll 0 (4th: 0: 0: 4th) row. 25 (26: 27: 28: 29) sts.

Work even until 18 (20: 20: 20: 22) rows less have been worked than on Back to start of shoulder shaping, ending with RS facing for next row.

Shape neck

Dec 1 st at end of next and foll 8 (8: 9: 9: 10) alt rows. 16 (17: 17: 18: 18) sts.

Work 1 (3: 1: 1: 1) rows, ending with RS facing for next row.

Shape shoulder

Bind off 8 (8: 8: 9: 9) sts at beg of next row.

Work 1 row.

Bind off rem 8 (9: 9: 9: 9) sts.

With RS facing, rejoin yarn to rem sts, bind off center 4 sts, K to last 2 sts, K2tog.

Complete to match first side, reversing shapings.

SLEEVES

Using size 10½ (7mm) needles and A, cast on 30 (30: 34: 34: 34) sts.

Work in rib as given for Back for 14 rows, inc 0 (1: 0: 0: 1) st at each end of last row and ending with RS facing for next row. 30 (32: 34: 34: 36) sts.

Break off A and join in MC.

Change to size 11 (8mm) needles.

Starting with a K row, work in St st, shaping sides by inc 1 st at each end of 5th (5th: 5th: 3rd: 5th) and every foll 6th row until there are 48 (50: 50: 56: 58) sts.

1ST, 2ND, AND 3RD SIZES ONLY

Inc 1 st at each end of every foll 8th row until there are 50 (52: 54: -: -) sts.

ALL SIZES

Work even until Sleeve measures 20½ (20½: 21: 21: 21¼)in/52 (52: 53: 53: 54)cm from cast-on edge, ending with RS facing for next row.

Shape top of sleeve

Bind off 4 sts at beg of next 2 rows. 42 (44: 46: 48: 50) sts.

Dec 1 st at each end of next 3 rows, then on foll 2 alt rows, then on foll 4th row. 30 (32: 34: 36: 38) sts.

Work 1 row.

Dec 1 st at each end of next and every foll alt row until 22 sts rem, then on foll 5 rows, ending with RS facing for next row.

Bind off rem 12 sts.

FINISHING

Press lightly on WS following instructions on yarn label. Sew shoulder seams.

Collar

With RS facing, using size 10½ (7mm) circular needle and A, starting and ending at base of front opening, pick up and knit 11 sts up right side of front opening to start of neck shaping, 22 (24: 24: 25: 26) sts up right side of neck, 24 (24: 24: 26: 28) sts from back, 22 (24: 24: 25: 26) sts down left side of neck, then 11 sts down left side of front opening. 90 (94: 94: 98: 102) sts.

Row 1 (RS of Collar, WS of body) P2, *K2, P2; rep from * to end.

This row sets position of rib as given for Back.

Work in rib for 2 rows more, ending with WS of Collar (RS of body) facing for next row.

Row 4 Rib 57 (59: 59: 62: 65), wrap next st (by slipping next st from left needle onto right needle, taking yarn to opposite side of work between needles and then slipping same st back onto left needle) and turn.

Row 5 Rib 24 (24: 24: 26: 28), wrap next st and turn.
Row 6 Rib 25 (25: 25: 27: 29), wrap next st and turn.
Row 7 Rib 26 (26: 26: 28: 30), wrap next st and turn.
Row 8 Rib 27 (27: 27: 29: 31), wrap next st and turn.
Row 9 Rib 28 (28: 28: 30: 32), wrap next st and turn.
Row 10 Rib 30 (30: 30: 32: 34), wrap next st and turn.
Row 11 Rib 32 (32: 32: 34: 36), wrap next st and turn.
Cont in this way, working an extra 2 sts on every row before wrapping next st and turning, until the foll row has been worked:
Next row (RS of Collar) Rib 68 (72: 72: 74: 80), wrap next st and turn.

Next row Rib to end.
Next row Rib 9, work 2 tog, yo (to make a buttonhole), rib to end.
Work in rib for 1 row more, ending with WS of Collar facing for next row.
Bind off loosely in rib.
Sew side and sleeve seams. Sew sleeves into armholes. Sew row-end edge of left front end of collar to bound-off sts at base of opening, then sew row-end edge of right front end in place on inside. Sew on toggle button.

CABLE SCARF

Martin Storey

SIZE

The finished scarf measures 7¾in/20cm by 72in/183cm.

YARNS

4 x 100g/3½oz balls of Rowan *Scottish Tweed Aran* in Rust 009

NEEDLES

Pair of size 6 (4mm) knitting needles
Pair of size 8 (5mm) knitting needles
Cable needle

GAUGE

20 sts and 26 rows to 4in/10cm measured over patt using size 8 (5mm) needles *or size to obtain correct gauge.*

ABBREVIATIONS

See page 133.

SPECIAL ABBREVIATIONS

Cr4R = slip next st onto cable needle and leave at back of work, K3, then K1 from cable needle; **Cr4L** = slip next 3 sts onto cable needle and leave at front of work, K1, then K3 from cable needle; **C6B** = slip next 3 sts onto cable needle and leave at back of work, K3, then K3 from cable needle.

SCARF

Using size 6 (4mm) needles, cast on 32 sts.
Work in garter st for 3 rows, ending with WS facing for next row.
Next row (WS) K5, M1, [K3, M1] 7 times, K6. 40 sts.
Change to size 8 (5mm) needles.
Work in patt as foll:
Row 1 (RS) Knit.
Row 2 K4, [P3, K2, P3, K4] 3 times.

Row 3 K4, [Cr4L, Cr4R, K4] 3 times.
Row 4 K5, [P6, K6] twice, P6, K5.
Row 5 K5, [C6B, K6] twice, C6B, K5.
Row 6 Rep row 4.
Row 7 K4, [Cr4R, Cr4L, K4] 3 times.
Row 8 Rep row 2.
Rows 9 to 16 Rep rows 1 and 2 four times.
These 16 rows form patt.
Cont in patt until Scarf measures approximately 71¼in/181cm, ending after a 9th patt row and with WS facing for next row.
Change to size 6 (4mm) needles.
Next row (WS) K5, K2tog, [K2, K2tog] 7 times, K5. 32 sts.
Work in garter st for 3 rows, ending with WS facing for next row.
Bind off knitwise (on WS).

FINISHING

Do NOT press.

SHAWL COLLAR JACKET

Wendy Baker

To fit chest					
40	42	44	46	48	in
102	107	112	117	122	cm
Finished measurements					
AROUND CHEST					
48½	50½	52¼	54¾	56½	in
123	128	133	139	144	cm
LENGTH TO BACK NECK					
26¾	27	27½	28	28¼	in
68	69	70	71	72	cm
SLEEVE SEAM					
19½	19½	20	20	20½	in
50	50	51	51	52	cm

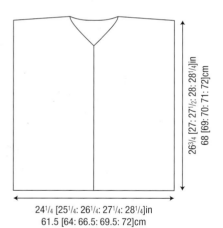

26¾ [27: 27½: 28: 28¼]in
68 [69: 70: 71: 72]cm

24¼ [25¼: 26¼: 27¼: 28¼]in
61.5 [64: 66.5: 69.5: 72]cm

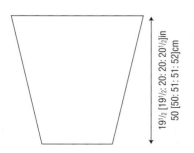

19½ [19½: 20: 20: 20½]in
50 [50: 51: 51: 52]cm

YARNS

14 (14: 15: 16: 16) x 100g/3½oz balls of Rowan *Scottish Tweed Chunky* in Lewis Grey 007

NEEDLES

Pair of size 10½ (7mm) knitting needles
Pair of size 11 (8mm) knitting needles
Cable needle

EXTRAS

6 buttons

GAUGE

15 sts and 16 rows to 4in/10cm measured over patt using size 11 (8mm) needles *or size to obtain correct gauge.*

ABBREVIATIONS

See page 133.

SPECIAL ABBREVIATIONS

C4B = slip next 2 sts onto cable needle and leave at back of work, K2, then K2 from cable needle; **C4F** = slip next 2 sts onto cable needle and leave at front of work, K2, then K2 from cable needle; **Cr4R** = slip next 2 sts onto cable needle and leave at back of work, K2, then P2 from cable needle; **Cr4L** = slip next 2 sts onto cable needle and leave at front of work, P2, then K2 from cable needle.

BACK

Using size 10½ (7mm) needles, cast on 77 (82: 87: 92: 97) sts.
Row 1 (RS) P2, *K3, P2; rep from * to end.
Row 2 K2, *P3, K2; rep from * to end.
These 2 rows form rib.
Work in rib for 15 rows more, ending with WS facing for next row.

Body chart

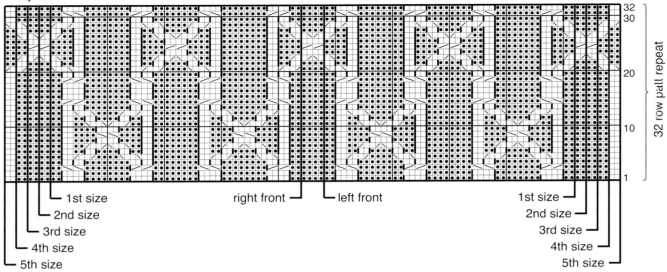

1st size
2nd size
3rd size
4th size
5th size

right front   left front

1st size
2nd size
3rd size
4th size
5th size

32 row patt repeat

Sleeve chart

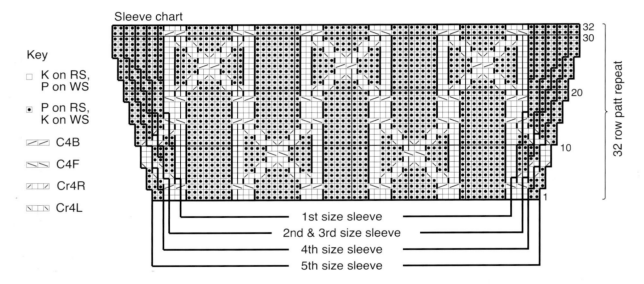

Key

☐ K on RS,
  P on WS

⊡ P on RS,
  K on WS

▨ C4B

◩ C4F

▧ Cr4R

◪ Cr4L

1st size sleeve
2nd & 3rd size sleeve
4th size sleeve
5th size sleeve

32 row patt repeat

Row 18 (WS) Rib 3 (2: 1: 2: 3), M1, [rib 5 (6: 7: 8: 9), M1] 14 (13: 12: 11: 10) times, rib to end. 92 (96: 100: 104: 108) sts.

Change to size 11 (8mm) needles.

Starting and ending rows as indicated and repeating the 32 row patt repeat throughout, now work in patt from chart for Body until Back measures 26½ (26¾: 27: 27½: 28)in/67 (68: 69: 70: 71)cm, ending with RS facing for next row.

Shape back neck and shoulders

Next row (RS) Patt 36 (38: 39: 40: 41) sts and turn, leaving rem sts on a holder.

Work each side of neck separately.

Bind off 4 sts at beg of next row, then 9 (10: 10: 11: 11) sts at beg of foll row.

Rep last 2 rows once more.

Work 1 row.

Bind off rem 10 (10: 11: 10: 11) sts.

With RS facing, rejoin yarn to rem sts, bind off center 20 (20: 22: 24: 26) sts, patt to end.

Complete to match first side, reversing shapings.

POCKET LININGS (make 2)

Using size 11 (8mm) needles, cast on 22 sts.

Starting with a P row, work in rev St st for 19 rows, ending with WS facing for next row.

Row 20 (WS) K6, M1, K10, M1, K6. 24 sts.
Break off yarn and leave sts on a holder.

LEFT FRONT

Using size 10½ (7mm) needles, cast on 37 (37: 42: 42: 47) sts.
Work in rib as given for Back for 17 rows, ending with WS facing for next row.
Row 18 (WS) Rib 3 (2: 3: 3: 5), M1, [rib 5 (4: 7: 5: 9), M1] 6 (8: 5: 7: 4) times, rib to end. 44 (46: 48: 50: 52) sts.
Change to size 11 (8mm) needles.
Starting and ending rows as indicated, now work in patt from chart for Body for 20 rows, ending with RS facing for next row.
Place pocket
Next row (RS) Patt 10 (11: 12: 13: 14) sts, slip next 24 sts onto a holder and, in their place, patt across 24 sts of first Pocket Lining, patt to end.
Work even until 16 (18: 18: 18: 20) rows less have been worked than on Back to start of shoulder shaping, ending with RS facing for next row.
Shape front slope
Keeping patt correct, dec 1 st at end of next row and at same edge on foll 15 (15: 16: 17: 18) rows. 28 (30: 31: 32: 33) sts.
Work 0 (2: 1: 0: 1) rows, ending with RS facing for next row.
Shape shoulder
Bind off 9 (10: 10: 11: 11) sts at beg of next and foll alt row.
Work 1 row.
Bind off rem 10 (10: 11: 10: 11) sts.

RIGHT FRONT

Work to match Left Front, reversing shapings and placement of pocket.

SLEEVES

Using size 10½ (7mm) needles, cast on 37 (42: 42: 42: 42) sts.
Starting with row 2, work in rib as given for Back for 18 rows, inc (dec: dec: dec: 0) 1 (2: 2: 2: 0) sts evenly across last row and ending with RS facing for next row. 38 (40: 40: 40: 42) sts.
Change to size 11 (8mm) needles.
Work in seed st as foll:

Row 1 (RS) *K1, P1; rep from * to end.

Row 2 *P1, K1; rep from * to end.

These 2 rows form seed st.

Cont in seed st, shaping sides by inc 1 st at each end of next and 6 (7: 7: 3: 5) foll 4th (4th: 4th: alt: alt) rows, then on 1 (0: 0: 6: 5) foll 6th (0: 0: 4th: 4th) rows. 54 (56: 56: 60: 64) sts.

Work 0 (2: 2: 0: 0) rows, ending with WS facing for next row.

Next row (WS) Seed st 6 (3: 3: 6: 8) sts, M1, [seed st 14 (10: 10: 16: 16) sts, M1] 3 (5: 5: 3: 3) times, seed st to end. 58 (62: 62: 64: 68) sts.

Starting and ending rows as indicated and repeating the 32 row patt repeat throughout, now work in patt from chart for Sleeve, shaping sides by inc 1 st at each end of 5th (5th: 5th: 3rd: 3rd) and every foll 6th (6th: 4th: 4th: 4th) row until there are 66 (70: 74: 78: 82) sts, taking inc sts into rev St st.

Work even until Sleeve measures 19½ (19½: 20: 20: 20½)in/50 (50: 51: 51: 52)cm from cast-on edge, ending with RS facing for next row.

Bind off in patt.

FINISHING

Press lightly on WS following instructions on yarn label. Sew shoulder seams.

Right front band and collar

Using size 10½ (7mm) needles, cast on 7 sts.

Work in garter st until Band, when slightly stretched, fits up right front opening edge from cast-on edge to start of front slope shaping, sewing in place as you go along and ending with RS facing for next row.

Shape for collar

Inc 1 st at end (attached edge) of next and every foll alt row until there are 19 sts.

Work 1 row, ending at straight (unattached) edge.

Next row K11 and turn.

Next row Sl 1, K to end.

Work 4 rows.

Rep last 6 rows until shorter row-end edge of Collar section, unstretched, fits up right front slope and across to center back neck, sewing in place as you go along. Bind off.

Mark positions for 6 buttons on this band—first to come in row 9, last to come just below start of front slope shaping, and rem 4 buttons evenly spaced between.

Left front band and collar

Using size 10½ (7mm) needles, cast on 7 sts.

Work in garter st for 8 rows, ending with RS facing for next row.

Row 9 (buttonhole row) (RS) K3, bind off 2 sts (to make a buttonhole—cast on 2 sts over these bound-off sts on next row), K to end.

Making 5 more buttonholes in this way to correspond with positions marked for buttons on Right Front Band, work even until this Band, when slightly stretched, fits up left front opening edge from cast-on edge to start of front slope shaping, sewing in place as you go along and ending with RS facing for next row.

Shape for collar

Inc 1 st at beg (attached edge) of next and every foll alt row until there are 19 sts, ending at straight (unattached) edge.

Next row K11 and turn.

Next row Sl 1, K to end.

Work 4 rows.

Rep last 6 rows until shorter row-end edge of Collar section, unstretched, fits up left front slope and across to center back neck, sewing in place as you go along. Bind off.

Sew center back seam of collar sections.

Pocket tops (both alike)

Slip 24 sts from pocket holder onto size 10½ (7mm) needles and rejoin yarn with RS facing.

Row 1 (RS) K6, K2tog, K8, K2tog, K6. 22 sts.

Work in garter st for 3 rows, ending with RS facing for next row.

Bind off.

Sew pocket linings in place on inside, then neatly sew down ends of pocket tops. Mark points along side seam edges of Back and Fronts 9¾ (10¼: 10½: 11: 11½)in/ 25 (26: 27: 28: 29)cm either side of shoulder seams, then sew bound-off edges of sleeves to Back and Fronts between these points. Sew side and sleeve seams. Sew on buttons.

TEXTURED SWEATER

Martin Storey

To fit chest

40	42	44	46	48	in
102	107	112	117	122	cm

Finished measurements

AROUND CHEST

47½	49¼	52	53½	56	in
121	125	132	136	142	cm

LENGTH TO BACK NECK

26	26½	26¾	27	27½	in
66	67	68	69	70	cm

SLEEVE SEAM

21	21	21¼	21¼	21½	in
53	53	54	54	55	cm

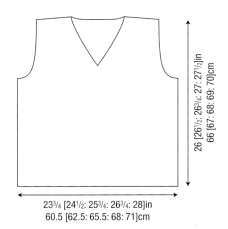

23¾ [24½: 25¾: 26¾: 28]in
60.5 [62.5: 65.5: 68: 71]cm

26 [26½: 26¾: 27: 27½]in
66 [67: 68: 69: 70]cm

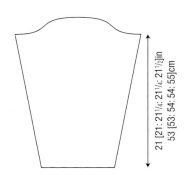

21 [21: 21¼: 21¼: 21½]in
53 [53: 54: 54: 55]cm

YARNS

Rowan *Scottish Tweed DK*:

MC	Celtic Mix 022	9 (10: 11: 11: 12) x 50g/1¾oz balls
A	Autumn 029	3 (4: 4: 4: 5) x 50g/1¾oz balls
B	Stormy Grey 004	3 (4: 4: 4: 5) x 50g/1¾oz balls

NEEDLES

Pair of size 3 (3.25mm) knitting needles
Pair of size 6 (4mm) knitting needles
Size 3 (3.25mm) circular knitting needle

GAUGE

19 sts and 34 rows to 4in/10cm measured over patt using size 6 (4mm) needles *or size to obtain correct gauge.*

ABBREVIATIONS

See page 133.

SPECIAL NOTE

While working patt, all slipped sts should be slipped purlwise with yarn at WS (back on RS rows, front on WS rows) of work.

BACK

Using size 3 (3.25mm) needles and MC, cast on 115 (119: 125: 129: 135) sts.

Work in garter st for 8 rows, ending with RS facing for next row.

Change to size 6 (4mm) needles.

Work in patt as foll:

Row 1 (RS) Using MC knit.

Row 2 Using MC purl.

Join in A.

Rows 3 and 4 Using A K1 (3: 2: 4: 3), sl 1, *K3, sl 1; rep from * to last 1 (3: 2: 4: 3) sts, K1 (3: 2: 4: 3).

Rows 5 and 6 Rep rows 1 and 2.

Join in B.

Rows 7 and 8 Using B K3 (1: 4: 2: 1), sl 1, *K3, sl 1; rep from * to last 3 (1: 4: 2: 1) sts, K3 (1: 4: 2: 1).

These 8 rows form patt.

Work in patt until Back measures 16½in/42cm from cast-on edge, ending with RS facing for next row.

Shape armholes

Keeping patt correct, bind off 6 sts at beg of next 2 rows. 103 (107: 113: 117: 123) sts.

Dec 1 st at each end of next and foll 5 alt rows. 91 (95: 101: 105: 111) sts.**

Work even until armhole measures 9½ (9¾: 10¼: 10½: 11)in/24 (25: 26: 27: 28)cm, ending with RS facing for next row.

Shape shoulders and back neck

Bind off 10 (11: 11: 12: 12) sts at beg of next 2 rows. 71 (73: 79: 81: 87) sts.

Next row (RS) Bind off 10 (11: 11: 12: 12) sts, patt until there are 14 (14: 16: 15: 17) sts on right needle and turn, leaving rem sts on a holder.

Work each side of neck separately.

Bind off 4 sts at beg of next row.

Bind off rem 10 (10: 12: 11: 13) sts.

With RS facing, rejoin yarns to rem sts, bind off center 23 (23: 25: 27: 29) sts, patt to end.

Complete to match first side, reversing shapings.

FRONT

Work as given for Back to **.

Work 5 rows, ending with RS facing for next row.

Divide for neck

Next row (RS) Patt 45 (47: 50: 52: 55) sts and turn, leaving rem sts on a holder.

Work each side of neck separately.

Keeping patt correct, dec 1 st at neck edge of 2nd and foll 2 (0: 1: 1: 1) alt rows, then on every foll 4th row until 30 (32: 34: 35: 37) sts rem.

Work even until Front matches Back to start of shoulder shaping, ending with RS facing for next row.

Shape shoulder

Bind off 10 (11: 11: 12: 12) sts at beg of next and foll alt row.

Work 1 row.

Bind off rem 10 (10: 12: 11: 13) sts.

With RS facing, slip center st onto a holder, rejoin yarns to rem sts, patt to end.

Complete to match first side, reversing shapings.

SLEEVES

Using size 3 (3.25mm) needles and MC, cast on 50 (54: 54: 54: 58) sts.

Row 1 (RS) K2, *P2, K2; rep from * to end.

Row 2 P2, *K2, P2; rep from * to end.

These 2 rows form rib.

Work in rib for 22 rows more, inc (dec: inc: inc: dec) 1 st at end of last row and ending with RS facing for next row. 51 (53: 55: 55: 57) sts.

Change to size 6 (4mm) needles.

Work in patt as foll:

Row 1 (RS) Using MC knit.

Row 2 Using MC purl.

Join in A.

Row 3 Using A [inc in first st] 0 (0: 0: 1: 1) times, K1 (2: 3: 2: 3), sl 1, *K3, sl 1; rep from * to last 1 (2: 3: 3: 4) sts, K1 (2: 3: 2: 3), [inc in last st] 0 (0: 0: 1: 1) times. 51 (53: 55: 57: 59) sts.

Row 4 Using A K1 (2: 3: 4: 5), sl 1, *K3, sl 1; rep from * to last 1 (2: 3: 4: 5) sts, K1 (2: 3: 4: 5).

Row 5 Using MC [inc in first st] 1 (1: 1: 0: 0) times, K to last 1 (1: 1: 0: 0) st, [inc in last st] 1 (1: 1: 0: 0) times. 53 (55: 57: 57: 59) sts.

Row 6 Using MC purl.

Join in B.

Row 7 Using B [inc in first st] 0 (0: 0: 1: 1) times, K4 (1: 2: 1: 2), sl 1, *K3, sl 1; rep from * to last 4 (1: 2: 2: 3) sts, K4 (1: 2: 1: 2), [inc in last st] 0 (0: 0: 1: 1) times. 53 (55: 57: 59: 61) sts.

Row 8 Using B K4 (1: 2: 3: 4), sl 1, *K3, sl 1; rep from * to last 4 (1: 2: 3: 4) sts, K4 (1: 2: 3: 4).

These 8 rows form patt and start sleeve shaping.

Cont in patt, shaping sides by inc 1 st at each end of 3rd (3rd: 3rd: 5th: 3rd) and every foll 6th (6th: 6th: 6th: 4th) row until there are 75 (85: 91: 103: 65) sts, taking inc sts into patt.

1ST, 2ND, 3RD, AND 5TH SIZES ONLY

Inc 1 st at each end of every foll 8th (8th: 8th: -: 6th) row until there are 91 (95: 99: -: 107) sts.

ALL SIZES

Work even until Sleeve measures 21 (21: 21¼: 21¼: 21½)in/53 (53: 54: 54: 55)cm from cast-on edge, ending with RS facing for next row.

Shape top of sleeve

Keeping patt correct, bind off 6 sts at beg of next 2 rows. 79 (83: 87: 91: 95) sts.

Dec 1 st at each end of 2nd row and 5 foll 3rd rows, then on foll row, ending with RS facing for next row.
Bind off rem 65 (69: 73: 77: 81) sts.

FINISHING

Press lightly on WS following instructions on yarn label.
Sew shoulder seams.

Neckband

With RS facing, using size 3 (3.25mm) circular needle and MC, starting and ending at left shoulder seam, pick up and knit 56 (60: 64: 68: 72) sts down left side of neck, K st on holder at base of V and mark this st with a colored thread, pick up and knit 56 (60: 64: 68: 72) sts up right side of neck, then 34 (34: 34: 38: 38) sts from back. 147 (155: 163: 175: 183) sts.

Round 1 (RS) *K2, P2; rep from * to within 4 sts of marked st, K2, K2tog tbl, K marked st, K2tog, **K2, P2; rep from ** to end.
This round sets position of rib as given for Sleeves.
Keeping rib correct as now set, cont as foll:
Round 2 Rib to within 2 sts of marked st, K2tog tbl, K marked st, K2tog, rib to end.
Rep last round 6 times more. 131 (139: 147: 159: 167) sts.
Bind off in rib, still decreasing either side of marked st as before.
Sew side and sleeve seams. Sew sleeves into armholes.

PLAIN GUERNSEY

Martin Storey

To fit chest

40	42	44	46	48	in
102	107	112	117	122	cm

Finished measurements

AROUND CHEST

48	50	52¼	54¼	56½	in
122	127	133	138	144	cm

LENGTH TO BACK NECK

26	26½	26¾	27	27½	in
66	67	68	69	70	cm

SLEEVE SEAM

20	20	20½	20½	20¾	in
51	51	52	52	53	cm

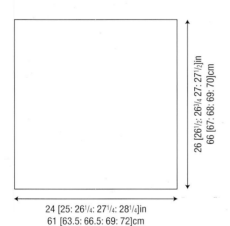

24 [25: 26¼: 27¼: 28¼]in
61 [63.5: 66.5: 69: 72]cm

26 [26½: 26¾: 27: 27½]in
66 [67: 68: 69: 70]cm

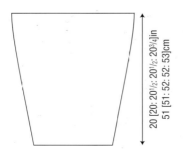

20 [20: 20½: 20½: 20¾]in
51 [51: 52: 52: 53]cm

YARNS

12 (13: 14: 14: 15) x 50g/1¾oz balls of Rowan *RYC Cashsoft DK* in Sage 516

NEEDLES

Pair of size 3 (3.25mm) knitting needles
Pair of size 6 (4mm) knitting needles
Size 3 (3.25mm) circular knitting needle

GAUGE

22 sts and 30 rows to 4in/10cm measured over St st using size 6 (4mm) needles *or size to obtain correct gauge.*

ABBREVIATIONS

See page 133.

BACK

Using size 3 (3.25mm) needles, cast on 134 (140: 146: 152: 158) sts.

Work in garter st for 18 rows, inc 0 (1: 0: 1: 0) st at each end of last row and ending with RS facing for next row. 134 (142: 146: 154: 158) sts.

Row 19 (RS) P2, *K2, P2; rep from * to end.
Row 20 K2, *P2, K2; rep from * to end.
These 2 rows form rib.

Work in rib for 4 rows more, dec 0 (1: 0: 1: 0) st at each end of last row and ending with RS facing for next row. 134 (140: 146: 152: 158) sts.

Change to size 6 (4mm) needles.

Starting with a K row, work in St st until Back measures 16½in/42cm from cast-on edge, ending with RS facing for next row.

Place markers at both ends of last row to denote base of armholes.

Next row (RS) Knit.
Next row P5, K5, P to last 10 sts, K5, P5.

Rep last 2 rows until work measures 9½ (9¾: 10¼: 10½: 11)in/24 (25: 26: 27: 28)cm *from markers*, ending with RS facing for next row.**

Shape back neck and shoulders

Next row (RS) K34 (37: 39: 41: 43) and slip these sts onto a holder, bind off next 66 (66: 68: 70: 72) sts, K to end.

Slip this second set of 34 (37: 39: 41: 43) sts onto another holder.

FRONT

Work as given for Back to **.

Join shoulder seams

Holding WS of Front against WS of Back, bind off first 34 (37: 39: 41: 43) sts of Front with first 34 (37: 39: 41: 43) sts of Back (by taking one st from Front with corresponding st from Back), bind off next 66 (66: 68: 70: 72) sts of Front *only*, then bind off rem 34 (37: 39: 41: 43) sts of Front with other set of 34 (37: 39: 41: 43) sts of Back to join second shoulder seam.

SLEEVES

Using size 3 (3.25mm) needles, cast on 62 (62: 66: 66: 66) sts.

Work in rib as given for Back for 32 rows, inc 0 (1: 0: 0: 1) st at each end of last row and ending with RS facing for next row. 62 (64: 66: 66: 68) sts.

Change to size 6 (4mm) needles.

Starting with a K row, work in St st, shaping sides by inc 1 st at each end of 3rd and every foll 4th row to 90 (98: 102: 114: 120) sts, then on every foll 6th row until there are 106 (110: 114: 118: 122) sts.

Work even until Sleeve measures 19¼ (19¼: 19½: 19½: 20)in/49 (49: 50: 50: 51)cm from cast-on edge, ending with RS facing for next row.

Starting with row 2, work in rib as given for Back for 6 rows, ending with RS facing for next row.

Bind off loosely in rib.

FINISHING

Press lightly on WS following instructions on yarn label.

Neck gussets (make 2)

Using size 6 (4mm) needles, cast on 15 sts.

Starting with a K row, work in St st, dec 1 st at each end of 2nd and foll 5 alt rows, ending with RS facing for next row. 3 sts.

Next row (RS) K3tog and fasten off.

Mark points along front and back neck bound-off edges 9 sts in from ends of shoulder seams. Matching fasten-off point of neck gusset to end of shoulder seam and ends of cast-on edge of neck gussets to marked points, sew neck gussets to front and back.

Neckband

With RS facing and using size 3 (3.25mm) circular needle, pick up and knit 15 sts from cast-on edge of left neck gusset, 49 (49: 51: 53: 55) sts from front, 15 sts from cast-on edge of right neck gusset, then 49 (49: 51: 53: 55) sts from back. 128 (128: 132: 136: 140) sts.

Round 1 (RS) *K2, P2; rep from * to end.

Rep this round 13 times more.

Bind off in rib.

Matching center of sleeve bound-off edge to shoulder seam, sew sleeves to back and front between markers. Mark points along sleeve and side seams 2in/5cm either side of underarm points. Sew sleeve seams below these points, then sew side seams below these points, leaving side seams open for first 18 rows. (There should now be a 4in/10cm "hole" in underarm seam.)

Underarm gussets (make 2)

Using size 6 (4mm) needles, cast on 12 sts.

Starting with a K row, work in St st for 16 rows, ending with RS facing for next row.

Bind off.

Matching corners of underarm gussets to "corners" of underarm "hole," sew underarm gussets in place so that, when sewn in place, gusset folds in half to form a triangle.

TEXTURED SCARF

Wendy Baker

SIZE

The finished scarf measures 11½in/29cm by 37½in/95cm.

YARNS

5 x 50g/1¾oz balls of Rowan *RYC Cashsoft DK* in either Donkey 517 or Thunder 518

NEEDLES

Pair of size 6 (4mm) knitting needles
Cable needle

GAUGE

25 sts and 34 rows to 4in/10cm measured over double seed st using size 6 (4mm) needles *or size to obtain correct gauge.*

ABBREVIATIONS

See page 133.

SPECIAL ABBREVIATIONS

C4B = slip next 2 sts onto cable needle and leave at back of work, K2, then K2 from cable needle; **C4F** = slip next 2 sts onto cable needle and leave at front of work, K2, then K2 from cable needle.

SCARF

Using size 6 (4mm) needles, cast on 73 sts.
Row 1 (RS) K1, *P1, K1; rep from * to end.
Rows 2 and 3 P1, *K1, P1; rep from * to end.
Row 4 Rep row 1.
These 4 rows form double seed st.
Work in double seed st for 4 rows more, ending with RS facing for next row.
Row 9 (RS) Seed st 13 sts, M1, [K2, M1] 5 times, seed st 27 sts, M1, [K2, M1] 5 times, seed st 13 sts. 85 sts.
Work in patt as foll:

Row 1 and every foll alt row (WS) Seed st 7 sts, K4, P20, K4, seed st 15 sts, K4, P20, K4, seed st 7 sts.

Row 2 Seed st 7 sts, P4, K6, C4B, C4F, K6, P4, seed st 15 sts, P4, K6, C4B, C4F, K6, P4, seed st 7 sts.

Row 4 Seed st 7 sts, P4, K4, C4B, K4, C4F, K4, P4, seed st 15 sts, P4, K4, C4B, K4, C4F, K4, P4, seed st 7 sts.

Row 6 Seed st 7 sts, P4, K2, C4B, K8, C4F, K2, P4, seed st 15 sts, P4, K2, C4B, K8, C4F, K2, P4, seed st 7 sts.

Row 8 Seed st 7 sts, P4, C4B, K12, C4F, P4, seed st 15 sts, P4, C4B, K12, C4F, P4, seed st 7 sts.

These 8 rows form patt.

Work in patt until Scarf measures 7¾in/20cm from cast-on edge, ending with RS facing for next row.

Divide for opening

Next row (RS) Patt 42 sts and turn, leaving rem sts on a holder.

Work each side separately.

Work in patt until Scarf measures 11¾in/30cm from cast-on edge, ending with WS facing for next row.

Break off yarn and leave these 42 sts on another holder.

With RS facing, rejoin yarn to rem sts, work 2 tog, patt to end. 42 sts.

Work in patt until Scarf measures 11¾in/30cm from cast-on edge, ending with WS facing for next row.

Join sections

Next row (WS) Patt first 41 sts of second section, inc in last st, then patt across 42 sts of first section. 85 sts.

Work in patt until Scarf measures 36¼in/92cm from cast-on edge, ending with WS facing for next row.

Next row (WS) Seed st 13 sts, P2tog, [P1, P2tog] 5 times, seed st 25 sts, P2tog, [P1, P2tog] 5 times, seed st 13 sts. 73 sts.

Work in double seed st across all sts for 7 rows, ending with WS facing for next row.

Bind off in patt (on WS).

FINISHING

Press lightly on WS following instructions on yarn label.

HERRINGBONE JACKET

Wendy Baker

To fit chest

40	42	44	46	48	in
102	107	112	117	122	cm

Finished measurements

AROUND CHEST

47½	49½	51½	53	55	in
121	126	131	135	140	cm

LENGTH TO BACK NECK

29	29½	30	30¼	30¾	in
74	75	76	77	78	cm

SLEEVE SEAM

21¼	21¼	21½	21½	22	in
54	54	55	55	56	cm

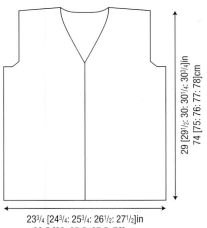

23¾ [24¾: 25¾: 26½: 27½]in
60.5 [63: 65.5: 67.5: 70]cm

29 [29½: 30: 30¼: 30¾]in
74 [75: 76: 77: 78]cm

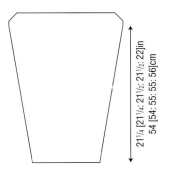

21¼ [21¼: 21½: 21½: 22]in
54 [54: 55: 55: 56]cm

YARNS

10 (11: 11: 12: 12) x 100g/3½oz balls of Rowan *Scottish Tweed Aran* in Storm Grey 004

NEEDLES

Pair of size 8 (5mm) knitting needles
Pair of size 9 (5.5mm) knitting needles

EXTRAS

4 buttons

GAUGE

17 sts and 23 rows to 4in/10cm measured over patt using size 9 (5.5mm) needles *or size to obtain correct gauge.*

ABBREVIATIONS

See page 133.

SPECIAL ABBREVIATIONS

KB1 = insert right needle point into loop running behind next st on left needle (this loop is top of st directly below next st on left needle) and K this loop, leaving st above on left needle, now K next st on left needle and slip st off left needle.

BACK

Using size 8 (5mm) needles, cast on 103 (107: 111: 115: 119) sts.

Work in garter st for 14 rows, ending with RS facing for next row.

Change to size 9 (5.5mm) needles.

Work in patt as foll:

Row 1 (RS) K2 (4: 6: 1: 3), *K2tog, K2, KB1, K2; rep from * to last 3 (5: 0: 2: 4) sts, K3 (5: 0: 2: 4).

Row 2 Purl.

Row 3 K3 (5: 0: 2: 4), *K2, KB1, K2, K2tog; rep from * to

last 2 (4: 6: 1: 3) sts, K2 (4: 6: 1: 3).

Row 4 Purl.

These 4 rows form patt.

Work in patt until Back measures 19½in/50cm from cast-on edge, ending with RS facing for next row.

Shape armholes

Keeping patt correct, bind off 5 sts at beg of next 2 rows. 93 (97: 101: 105: 109) sts.

Next row (RS) K1, sl 1, K1, psso, patt to last 3 sts, K2tog, K1.

Working all decreases as set by last row, dec 1 st at each end of 2nd and foll 2 alt rows. 85 (89: 93: 97: 101) sts.

Work even until armhole measures 9 (9½: 9¾: 10¼: 10½)in/23 (24: 25: 26: 27)cm, ending with RS facing for next row.

Shape back neck and shoulders

Next row (RS) Patt 28 (30: 31: 32: 33) sts and turn, leaving rem sts on a holder.

Work each side of neck separately.

Dec 1 st at neck edge of next row.

Bind off 13 (14: 14: 15: 15) sts at beg and dec 1 st at end of next row.

Work 1 row.

Bind off rem 13 (14: 15: 15: 16) sts.

With RS facing, rejoin yarn to rem sts, bind off center 29 (29: 31: 33: 35) sts, patt to end.

Complete to match first side, reversing shapings.

POCKET LININGS (make 2)

Using size 9 (5.5mm) needles, cast on 28 sts.

Starting with a K row, work in St st for 40 rows, ending with RS facing for next row.

Break off yarn and leave sts on a holder.

LEFT FRONT

Using size 8 (5mm) needles, cast on 54 (56: 58: 60: 62) sts.

Work in garter st for 13 rows, ending with WS facing for next row.

Row 14 (WS) K10 and slip these sts onto a holder, M1, K to end. 45 (47: 49: 51: 53) sts.

Change to size 9 (5.5mm) needles.

Work in patt as foll:

Row 1 (RS) K2 (4: 6: 1: 3), *K2tog, K2, KB1, K2; rep from * to last st, K1.

Row 2 Purl.

Row 3 K3 (5: 0: 2: 4), *K2, KB1, K2, K2tog; rep from * to end.

Row 4 Purl.

These 4 rows form patt.

Work in patt for 32 rows more, ending with RS facing for next row.

Place pocket

Next row (RS) Patt 10 (11: 12: 13: 14) sts, slip next 28 sts onto a holder and, in their place, patt across 28 sts of first Pocket Lining, patt to end.

Cont in patt until Left Front matches Back to start of armhole shaping, ending with RS facing for next row.

Shape armhole

Keeping patt correct, bind off 5 sts at beg of next row. 40 (42: 44: 46: 48) sts.

Work 1 row.

Shape front slope

Keeping patt correct and working all armhole decreases as set by Back, dec 1 st at armhole edge of next and foll 3 alt rows *and at the same time* dec 1 st at front slope edge of next and foll 4th row. 34 (36: 38: 40: 42) sts.

Dec 1 st at front slope edge *only* on 2nd and 2 (1: 3: 5: 7) foll 4th rows, then on 5 (6: 5: 4: 3) foll 6th rows. 26 (28: 29: 30: 31) sts.

Work even until Left Front matches Back to start of shoulder shaping, ending with RS facing for next row.

Shape shoulder

Bind off 13 (14: 14: 15: 15) sts at beg of next row.

Work 1 row.

Bind off rem 13 (14: 15: 15: 16) sts.

RIGHT FRONT

Using size 8 (5mm) needles, cast on 54 (56: 58: 60: 62) sts.

Work in garter st for 13 rows, ending with WS facing for next row.

Row 14 (WS) K to last 10 sts, M1 and turn, leaving rem 10 sts on a holder. 45 (47: 49: 51: 53) sts.

Change to size 9 (5.5mm) needles.

Work in patt as foll:

Row 1 (RS) *K2tog, K2, KB1, K2; rep from * to last 3 (5: 0: 2: 4) sts, K3 (5: 0: 2: 4).

Row 2 Purl.

Row 3 K1, *K2, KB1, K2, K2tog; rep from * to last 2 (4: 6: 1: 3) sts, K2 (4: 6: 1: 3).

Row 4 Purl.

These 4 rows form patt.

Work in patt for 32 rows more, ending with RS facing for next row.

Place pocket

Next row (RS) Patt 7 (8: 9: 10: 11) sts, slip next 28 sts onto a holder and, in their place, patt across 28 sts of second Pocket Lining, patt to end.

Complete to match Left Front, reversing shapings.

SLEEVES

Using size 8 (5mm) needles, cast on 45 (47: 49: 49: 51) sts.

Work in garter st for 14 rows, ending with RS facing for next row.

Change to size 9 (5.5mm) needles.

Work in patt as foll:

Row 1 (RS) K1 (2: 3: 3: 4), *K2tog, K2, KB1, K2; rep from * to last 2 (3: 4: 4: 5) sts, K2 (3: 4: 4: 5).

Row 2 Purl.

Row 3 [Inc in first st] 0 (0: 0: 1: 1) times, K2 (3: 4: 3: 4), *K2, KB1, K2, K2tog; rep from * to last 1 (2: 3: 3: 4) sts, K1 (2: 3: 2: 3), [inc in last st] 0 (0: 0: 1: 1) times. 45 (47: 49: 51: 53) sts.

Row 4 Purl.

These 4 rows form patt and start sleeve shaping.

Cont in patt, shaping sides by inc 1 st at each end of next (next: next: 3rd: 3rd) and every foll 6th (6th: 6th: 6th: 4th) row until there are 71 (73: 81: 85: 59) sts, taking inc sts into St st until there are sufficient to work in patt.

1ST, 2ND, 3RD, AND 5TH SIZES ONLY

Inc 1 st at each end of every foll 8th (8th: 8th: -: 6th) row until there are 77 (79: 83: -: 89) sts.

ALL SIZES

Work even until Sleeve measures 21¼ (21¼: 21½: 21½: 22)in/54 (54: 55: 55: 56)cm from cast-on edge, ending with RS facing for next row.

Shape top of sleeve

Place markers at both ends of last row to denote top of sleeve seam.

Work 4 rows, ending with RS facing for next row.

Working all decreases in same way as for armhole, dec 1 st at each end of next and foll 3 alt rows.

Work 1 row, ending with RS facing for next row.

Bind off rem 69 (71: 75: 77: 81) sts.

FINISHING

Press lightly on WS following instructions on yarn label. Sew shoulder seams. Mark points along front slope edges 3½in/9cm down from shoulder seams.

Right front band and collar

Slip 10 sts from right front holder onto size 8 (5mm) needles and rejoin yarn with WS facing.

Row 1 (WS) Inc in first st, K9. 11 sts.

Work in garter st until Band, when slightly stretched, fits up right front opening edge to start of front slope shaping, sewing in place as you go along and ending with RS facing for next row.

Shape for collar

Inc 1 st at beg (unattached edge) of next and every foll 4th row until there are 21 sts.

Work even until Collar section, unstretched, fits up right front slope to marked point, sewing in place as you go along and ending at shaped (unattached) edge.

Next row Bind off 8 sts, then cast on 8 sts, K to end.

**Work 5 rows.

Next row K12 and turn.

Next row Sl 1, K11.

Work 1 row.

Rep from ** until shorter row-end edge of Collar section, unstretched, fits up remainder of right front slope and across to center back neck, sewing in place as you go along.

Bind off.

Mark positions for 4 buttons on this band—first to come in row 15, last to come just below start of front slope shaping, and rem 2 buttons evenly spaced between.

Left front band and collar

Slip 10 sts from left front holder onto size 8 (5mm) needles and rejoin yarn with RS facing.

Next row (RS) Inc in first st, K1, bind off 2 sts (to make a buttonhole—cast on 2 sts over these bound-off sts on next row), K to end. 11 sts.

Making 3 more buttonholes in this way to correspond with positions marked for buttons on Left Front Band, work even in garter st until this Band, when slightly stretched, fits up left front opening edge to start of front slope shaping, sewing in place as you go along and ending with RS facing for next row.

Shape for collar

Inc 1 st at end (unattached edge) of next and every foll 4th row until there are 21 sts.

Complete to match Right Front Band and Collar, reversing shapings.

Sew center back seam of collar sections.

Pocket tops (both alike)

Slip 28 sts from pocket holder onto size 8 (5mm) needles and rejoin yarn with RS facing.

Work in garter st for 6 rows, ending with RS facing for next row.

Bind off.

Sew pocket linings in place on inside, then neatly sew down ends of pocket tops. Matching center of bound-off edge of sleeve to shoulder seam and sleeve markers to top of side seam, sew sleeves into armholes. Sew side and sleeve seams. Sew on buttons.

DIAMOND GANSEY

Martin Storey

To fit chest

40	42	44	46	48	in
102	107	112	117	122	cm

Finished measurements

AROUND CHEST

48	50	52¼	54¼	56½	in
122	127	133	138	144	cm

LENGTH TO BACK NECK

26	26½	26¾	27	27½	in
66	67	68	69	70	cm

SLEEVE SEAM

20¾	20¾	21¼	21¼	21½	in
53	53	54	54	55	cm

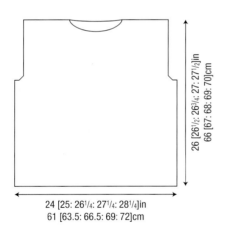

24 [25: 26¼: 27¼: 28¼]in
61 [63.5: 66.5: 69: 72]cm

26 [26½: 26¾: 27: 27½]in
66 [67: 68: 69: 70]cm

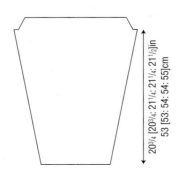

20¾ [20¾: 21¼: 21¼: 21½]in
53 [53: 54: 54: 55]cm

YARNS

14 (15: 16: 16: 17) x 50g/1¾oz balls of Rowan *Pure Wool DK* in Glade 021

NEEDLES

Pair of size 3 (3.25mm) knitting needles
Pair of size 6 (4mm) knitting needles
Size 3 (3.25mm) circular knitting needle

GAUGE

22 sts and 30 rows to 4in/10cm measured over St st using size 6 (4mm) needles *or size to obtain correct gauge.*

ABBREVIATIONS

See page 133.

SPECIAL NOTE

Armhole shaping is NOT shown on chart.

BACK

Using size 3 (3.25mm) needles, cast on 134 (140: 146: 152: 158) sts.
Work in garter st for 8 rows, ending with RS facing for next row.
Change to size 6 (4mm) needles.
Starting and ending rows as indicated, working chart rows 1 to 8, 11 times, then chart rows 9 to 78 once only and then repeating chart rows 78 to 82 as required, work in patt from chart as foll:
Work even until Back measures 16½in/42cm from cast-on edge, ending with RS facing for next row.

Shape armholes

Keeping patt correct, bind off 6 sts at beg of next 2 rows. 122 (128: 134: 140: 146) sts.
Dec 1 st at each end of next and foll 5 alt rows. 110 (116: 122: 128: 134) sts.

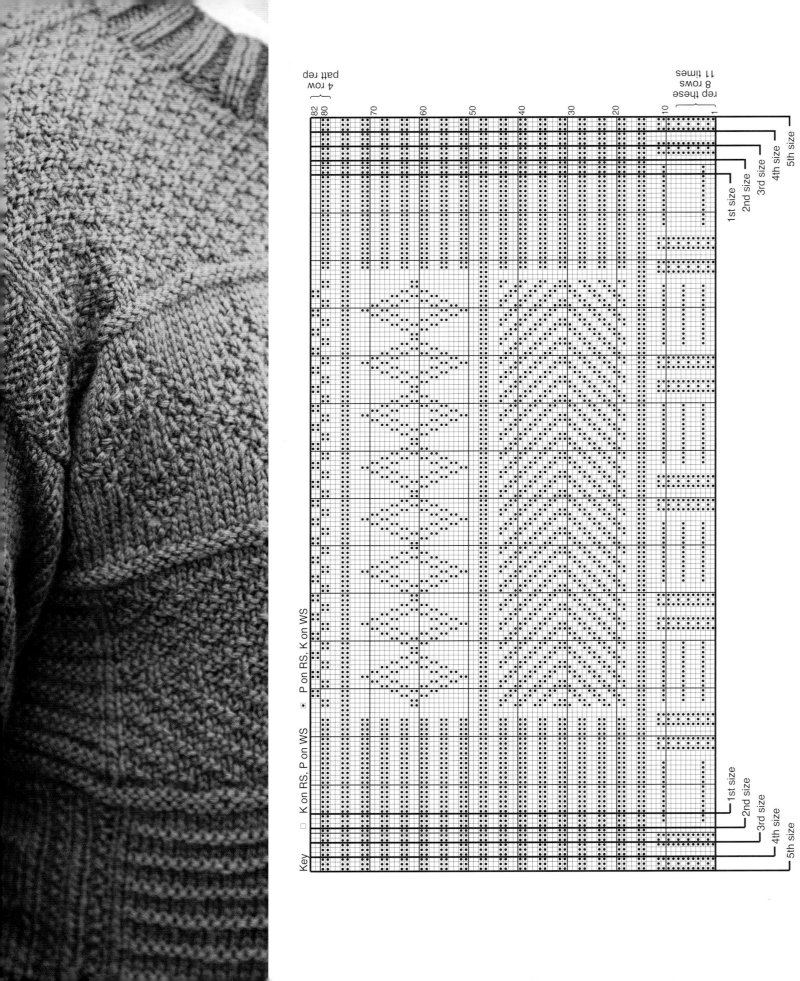

Work even until armhole measures 9 (9½: 9¾: 10¼: 10½)in/23 (24: 25: 26: 27)cm, ending with RS facing for next row.

Shape back neck and shoulders

Next row (RS) Patt 34 (37: 39: 41: 43) sts and turn, leaving rem sts on a holder.

Work each side of neck separately.

Dec 1 st at neck edge of next row, ending with RS facing for next row.

Break off yarn and leave rem 33 (36: 38: 40: 42) sts on a holder.

With RS facing, rejoin yarn to rem sts, bind off center 42 (42: 44: 46: 48) sts, patt to end.

Dec 1 st at neck edge of next row, ending with RS facing for next row.

Break off yarn and leave rem 33 (36: 38: 40: 42) sts on a holder.

FRONT

Work as given for Back until 16 (18: 18: 18: 20) rows less have been worked than on Back to sts left on shoulder holders, ending with RS facing for next row.

Shape neck

Next row (RS) Patt 40 (44: 46: 48: 51) sts and turn, leaving rem sts on a holder.

Work each side of neck separately.

Keeping patt correct, dec 1 st at neck edge of next 4 rows, then on foll 2 (3: 3: 3: 4) alt rows, then on foll 4th row. 33 (36: 38: 40: 42) sts.

Work 3 rows, ending with RS facing for next row.

Join shoulder seam

Holding WS of Front against WS of Back, bind off sts of left front shoulder seam with corresponding sts of left back shoulder seam (by taking one st of Front with corresponding st of Back).

With RS facing, rejoin yarn to rem sts, bind off center 30 (28: 30: 32: 32) sts, patt to end.

Keeping patt correct, dec 1 st at neck edge of next 4 rows, then on foll 2 (3: 3: 3: 4) alt rows, then on foll 4th row. 33 (36: 38: 40: 42) sts.

Work 3 rows, ending with RS facing for next row.

Join shoulder seam

Holding WS of Front against WS of Back, bind off sts of right front shoulder seam with corresponding sts of right back shoulder seam (by taking one st of Front with corresponding st of Back).

SLEEVES

Using size 3 (3.25mm) needles, cast on 54 (58: 58: 58: 62) sts.

Row 1 (RS) K2, *P2, K2; rep from * to end.

Row 2 P2, *K2, P2; rep from * to end.

These 2 rows form rib.

Work in rib for 26 rows more, inc 1 (0: 1: 1: 0) st at each end of last row and ending with RS facing for next row. 56 (58: 60: 60: 62) sts.

Change to size 6 (4mm) needles.

Work in patt as foll:

Row 1 (RS) K24 (25: 26: 26: 27), P1, K1, P1, K2, P1, K1, P1, K to end.

Row 2 P24 (25: 26: 26: 27), K3, P2, K3, P to end.

These 2 rows form patt.

Work in patt, shaping sides by inc 1 st at each end of next and every foll 4th row to 88 (96: 102: 114: 118) sts, then on every foll 6th row until there are 106 (110: 114: 118: 122) sts, taking inc sts into St st.

Work even until Sleeve measures 20¾ (20¾: 21¼: 21¼: 21½)in/53 (53: 54: 54: 55)cm from cast-on edge, ending with RS facing for next row.

Shape top of sleeve

Keeping patt correct, bind off 6 sts at beg of next 2 rows. 94 (98: 102: 106: 110) sts.

Dec 1 st at each end of next and foll 5 alt rows, then on foll row, ending with RS facing for next row.

Bind off rem 80 (84: 88: 92: 96) sts.

FINISHING

Press lightly on WS following instructions on yarn label.

Neckband

With RS facing and using size 3 (3.25mm) circular needle, starting and ending at left shoulder seam, pick up and knit 18 (19: 19: 21: 22) sts down left side of neck, 30 (28: 30: 32: 32) sts from front, 18 (19: 19: 21: 22) sts up right side of neck, then 46 (46: 48: 50: 52) sts from back. 112 (112: 116: 124: 128) sts.

Round 1 (RS) *K2, P2; rep from * to end.

Rep this round until Neckband measures 2in/5cm.

Bind off in rib.

Sew sleeves into armholes. Sew side and sleeve seams.

FAIR ISLE STRIPE SWEATER

Wendy Baker

To fit chest

40	42	44	46	48	in
102	107	112	117	122	cm

Finished measurements

AROUND CHEST

47¼	49¼	51½	53½	56	in
120	125	131	136	142	cm

LENGTH TO BACK NECK

26½	26¾	27½	28	28¾	in
67	68	70	71	73	cm

SLEEVE SEAM

19½	19½	20	20	20½	in
50	50	51	51	52	cm

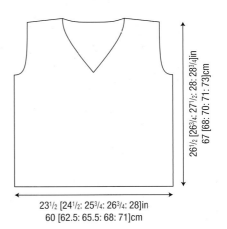

23½ [24½: 25¾: 26¾: 28]in
60 [62.5: 65.5: 68: 71]cm

26½ [26¾: 27½: 28: 28¾]in
67 [68: 70: 71: 73]cm

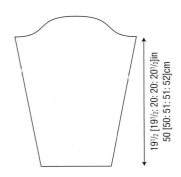

19½ [19½: 20: 20: 20½]in
50 [50: 51: 51: 52]cm

YARNS

Rowan *Wool Cotton*:

MC	Misty 903	7 (8: 9: 9: 10) x 50g/1¾oz balls
A	Inky 908	2 (2: 2: 3: 3) x 50g/1¾oz balls
B	Elf 946	2 (2: 2: 3: 3) x 50g/1¾oz balls
C	Deepest Olive 907	2 (2: 2: 3: 3) x 50g/1¾oz balls
D	Citron 901	2 (2: 2: 3: 3) x 50g/1¾oz balls
E	Moonstone 961	2 (2: 2: 3: 3) x 50g/1¾oz balls

NEEDLES

Pair of size 5 (3.75mm) knitting needles
Pair of size 6 (4mm) knitting needles
Size 5 (3.75mm) circular knitting needle

GAUGE

22 sts and 30 rows to 4in/10cm measured over St st using size 6 (4mm) needles *or size to obtain correct gauge.*

ABBREVIATIONS

See page 133.

SPECIAL NOTE

When working patt from chart, strand yarn not in use loosely across WS of work. When working chart rows 1 to 107 for first time, work odd-numbered rows as RS (K) rows, reading them from right to left, and even-numbered rows as WS (P) rows, reading them from left to right. On following rep of chart, work odd-numbered rows as WS (P) rows, reading them from left to right, and even-numbered rows as RS (K) rows, reading them from right to left.

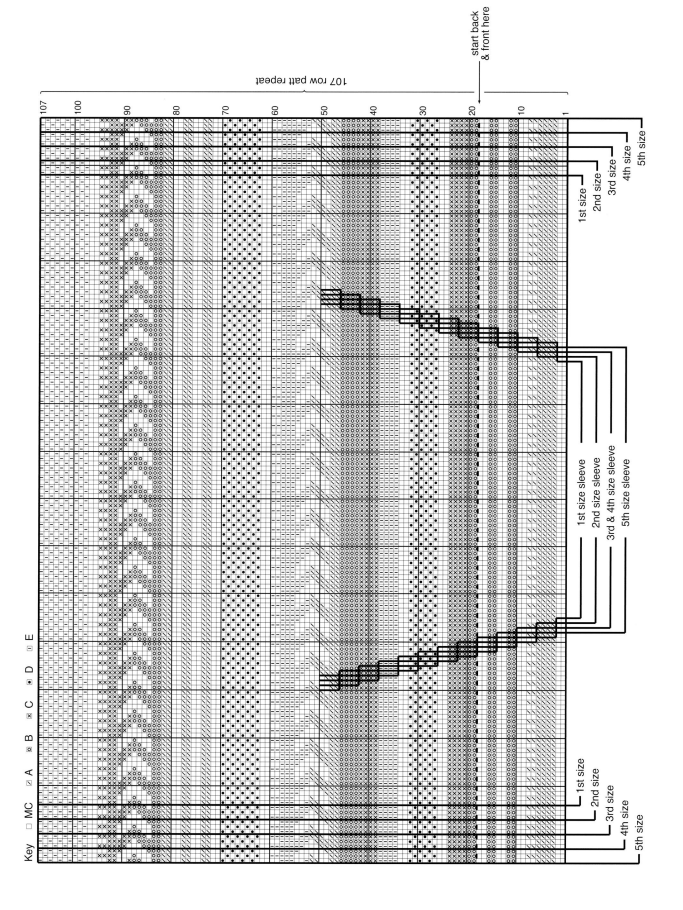

BACK

Using size 5 (3.75mm) needles and MC, cast on 130 (138: 142: 150: 154) sts.

Row 1 (RS) K2, *P2, K2; rep from * to end.

Row 2 P2, *K2, P2; rep from * to end.

These 2 rows form rib.

Joining in and breaking off colors as required, work in rib in stripes as foll:

Rows 3 and 4 Using D.

Rows 5 and 6 Using MC.

Rows 7 to 10 Using A.

Rows 11 and 12 Using MC and inc 1 (0: 1: 0: 1) st at each end of last row. 132 (138: 144: 150: 156) sts.

Change to size 6 (4mm) needles.

Starting and ending rows as indicated, joining in and breaking off colors as required and repeating the 107 row patt repeat throughout, now work in patt from chart as foll:

Starting with chart row 19, work even until Back measures 17¼ (17¼: 17¾: 17¾: 18)in/44 (44: 45: 45: 46)cm, ending with RS facing for next row.

Shape armholes

Keeping patt correct, bind off 6 sts at beg of next 2 rows. 120 (126: 132: 138: 144) sts.**

Dec 1 st at each end of next and foll 4 alt rows. 110 (116: 122: 128: 134) sts.

Work even until armhole measures 8¼ (8½: 9: 9½: 9¾)in/21 (22: 23: 24: 25)cm, ending with RS facing for next row.

Shape back neck

Next row (RS) Patt 36 (39: 41: 43: 45) sts and turn, leaving rem sts on a holder.

Work each side of neck separately.

Keeping patt correct, dec 1 st at neck edge of next 3 rows. 33 (36: 38: 40: 42) sts.

Work 2 rows, ending with RS facing for next row.

Shape shoulder

Bind off 11 (12: 13: 13: 14) sts at beg of next and foll alt row.

Work 1 row.

Bind off rem 11 (12: 12: 14: 14) sts.

With RS facing, rejoin yarns to rem sts, bind off center 38 (38: 40: 42: 44) sts, patt to end.

Complete to match first side, reversing shapings.

FRONT

Work as given for Back to **.

Divide for neck

Next row (RS) K2tog, patt 57 (60: 63: 66: 69) sts and turn, leaving rem sts on a holder.

Work each side of neck separately.

Keeping patt correct, dec 1 st at each end of 2nd and foll 3 alt rows. 50 (53: 56: 59: 62) sts.

Dec 1 st at neck edge **only** of 2nd and foll 8 (7: 7: 8: 8) alt rows, then on every foll 4th row until 33 (36: 38: 40: 42) sts rem.

Work even until Front matches Back to start of shoulder shaping, ending with RS facing for next row.

Shape shoulder

Bind off 11 (12: 13: 13: 14) sts at beg of next and foll alt row.

Work 1 row.

Bind off rem 11 (12: 12: 14: 14) sts.

With RS facing, slip center 2 sts onto a holder, rejoin yarns to rem sts, patt to last 2 sts, K2tog.

Complete to match first side, reversing shapings.

SLEEVES

Using size 5 (3.75mm) needles and MC, cast on 54 (54: 58: 58: 58) sts.

Work striped rib rows 1 to 10 as given for Back.

Using MC work in rib for 2 rows more, inc 0 (1: 0: 0: 1) st at each end of last row and ending with RS facing for next row. 54 (56: 58: 58: 60) sts.

Change to size 6 (4mm) needles.

Starting and ending rows as indicated and starting with chart row 1, now work in patt from chart as foll:

Inc 1 st at each end of 3rd and every foll 4th row to 80 (88: 94: 106: 110) sts, then on every foll 6th row until there are 104 (108: 112: 116: 120) sts, taking inc sts into patt.

Work even until Sleeve measures approximately 19½ (19½: 20: 20: 20½)in/50 (50: 51: 51: 52)cm from cast-on edge, ending after same patt row as on Back to start of armhole shaping and with RS facing for next row.

Shape top of sleeve

Keeping patt correct, bind off 6 sts at beg of next 2 rows. 92 (96: 100: 104: 108) sts.

Dec 1 st at each end of next and foll 4 alt rows. 82 (86: 90: 94: 98) sts.

Work 1 row, ending with RS facing for next row.

Bind off 4 sts at beg of next 16 rows.
Bind off rem 18 (22: 26: 30: 34) sts.

FINISHING

Press lightly on WS following instructions on yarn label.
Sew shoulder seams.

Neckband

With RS facing, using size 5 (3.75mm) circular needle
and MC, pick up and knit 64 (64: 68: 68: 72) sts down
left side of neck, K 2 sts left on holder at base of V and
place a marker between these sts, pick up and knit 64
(64: 68: 68: 72) sts up right side of neck, then 54 (54: 58:
58: 62) sts from Back. 184 (184: 196: 196: 208) sts.

Round 1 (RS) *K2, P2; rep from * to end.

This round sets position of rib as given for Back.

Keeping rib correct as now set, cont as foll:

Round 2 Rib to within 2 sts of marker, K2tog, slip marker
onto right needle, sl 1, K1, psso, rib to end.

Round 3 Rib to within 1 st of marker, K2 (marker is
between these 2 sts), rib to end.

Rounds 4 to 7 Rep rounds 2 and 3 twice. 178 (178: 190:
190: 202) sts.

Break off MC and join in A.

Rounds 8 and 9 Rep rounds 2 and 3 but using A.
176 (176: 188: 188: 200) sts.

Bind off in rib, still decreasing either side of marker
as before.

Sew sleeves into armholes. Sew side and sleeve seams.

BIRD'S-EYE SOCKS

Martin Storey

SIZE

The finished socks measure 10½in/27cm from heel
to toe.

YARNS

2 x 50g/1¾oz balls of Rowan *Felted Tweed* in **MC**
(Treacle 145) and 1 ball in **A** (Camel 157)

NEEDLES

Set of 4 double-pointed size 5 (3.75mm) knitting
needles

GAUGE

23 sts and 32 rows to 4in/10cm measured over St st
using size 5 (3.75mm) needles or size to obtain correct
gauge.

ABBREVIATIONS

See page 133.

SOCKS (both alike)

Using size 5 (3.75mm) needles and MC, cast on
80 sts.
Distribute these 80 sts evenly over 3 needles.
Working in rounds, work as foll:
Round 1 (RS) *K1, P1; rep from * to end.
This round forms rib.
Work in rib for 3 rounds more.
Join in A.
Stranding yarn not in use loosely across WS of work,
work in patt as foll:
Rounds 1 and 2 (RS) Using MC knit.
Round 3 *Using MC K1, using A K1; rep from * to end.
These 3 rounds form patt.
Work in patt until Sock measures 3½in/9cm from cast-on
edge, ending after patt round 2.
Break off A and cont using MC only.

Work in rib until sock measures 6½in/17cm from
cast-on edge.
This completes cuff and turn-back.
Turn work at end of last round and turn Sock inside out
to reverse RS of work.
Round 1 (RS) Knit.
This round forms St st.
Work in St st for 3 rounds more.
Round 5 K9, K2tog, K to last 11 sts, sl 1, K1, psso, K9.
78 sts.
Work 7 rounds.
Round 13 K8, K2tog, K to last 10 sts, sl 1, K1, psso, K8.
76 sts.
Work 7 rounds.
Round 21 K7, K2tog, K to last 9 sts, sl 1, K1, psso, K7.
74 sts.
Work 7 rounds.
Round 29 K6, K2tog, K to last 8 sts, sl 1, K1, psso, K6.
72 sts.
Work 7 rounds.
Round 37 K5, K2tog, K to last 7 sts, sl 1, K1, psso, K5.
70 sts.
Work 7 rounds.
Round 45 K4, K2tog, K to last 6 sts, sl 1, K1, psso, K4.
68 sts.
Work 7 rounds.
Round 53 K7, K2tog, K15, K2tog, [K15, sl 1, K1, psso]
twice, K8. 64 sts.
Break off yarn.
Shape heel
Slip first and last 18 sts of last round onto one needle,
leaving rem 28 sts on a holder.
Starting with a K row, rejoin yarn to these 36 heel sts
with RS facing and work back and forth in rows of St st
as foll:
Work 20 rows, ending with RS facing for next row.
Row 21 (RS) K26, sl 1, K1, psso and turn.

Row 22 Sl 1, P16, P2tog and turn.

Row 23 Sl 1, K16, sl 1, K1, psso and turn.

Rep rows 22 and 23 seven times more, then row 22 again, ending with RS facing for next row. 18 sts.

Break off yarn and slip first 9 sts of heel onto another holder.

Rejoin yarn and with RS facing, work as foll: K last 9 heel sts, pick up and knit 15 sts down first row-end edge of heel, K first st left on first holder, place marker on right needle, K next 26 sts, place second marker on right needle, then K last st from first holder, pick up and knit 15 sts up other row-end edge of heel, then K 9 sts from heel holder. 76 sts.

Distribute sts evenly over 3 needles and complete foot in rounds as foll:

Next round Knit.

Next round K to within 2 sts of first marker, K2tog, slip marker onto right needle, K26, slip 2nd marker onto right needle, K2tog tbl, K to end.

Rep last 2 rounds 5 times more. 64 sts.

Work even until foot section measures 8¼in/21cm from back of heel.

Shape toe

Counting in from both ends of last round, place markers on needles after 16th st from each end of round. (There will be 32 sts between markers.)

Round 1 [K to within 3 sts of marker, K2tog, K2 (marker is between these 2 sts), sl 1, K1, psso] twice, K to end.

Round 2 Knit.

Rep last 2 rounds 8 times more. 28 sts.

Break off yarn.

Slip first and last 7 sts of last round onto one needle, and rem 14 sts onto another needle. Turn Sock WS out and hold needles together so that right sides of toe are facing each other. Rejoin yarn and join toe seam by binding off both sets of 14 sts together (by taking one st from front needle with corresponding st from back needle).

FINISHING

Press lightly on WS following instructions on yarn label.

CABLE SWEATER

Martin Storey

To fit chest					
40	42	44	46	48	in
102	107	112	117	122	cm

Finished measurements

AROUND CHEST

48¾	51	52¾	55	56½	in
124	130	134	140	144	cm

LENGTH TO BACK NECK

26	26½	26¾	27	27½	in
66	67	68	69	70	cm

SLEEVE SEAM

20½	20½	21	21	21¼	in
52	52	53	53	54	cm

YARNS

11 (12: 12: 13: 13) x 100g/3½oz balls of Rowan *Scottish Tweed Aran* in Lovat 033

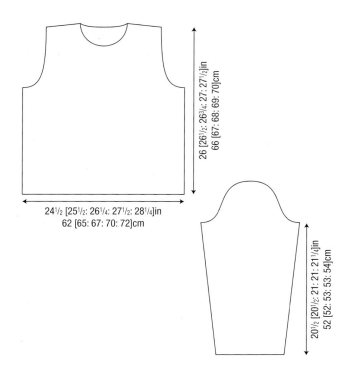

24½ [25½: 26¼: 27½: 28¼]in
62 [65: 67: 70: 72]cm

26 [26½: 26¾: 27: 27½]in
66 [67: 68: 69: 70]cm

20½ [20½: 21: 21: 21¼]in
52 [52: 53: 53: 54]cm

NEEDLES

Pair of size 6 (4mm) knitting needles
Pair of size 8 (5mm) knitting needles
Cable needle

GAUGE

20 sts and 26 rows to 4in/10cm measured over patt using size 8 (5mm) needles *or size to obtain correct gauge.*

ABBREVIATIONS

See page 133.

SPECIAL ABBREVIATIONS

Cr4R = slip next st onto cable needle and leave at back of work, K3, then K1 from cable needle; **Cr4L** = slip next 3 sts onto cable needle and leave at front of work, K1, then K3 from cable needle; **C6B** = slip next 3 sts onto cable needle and leave at back of work, K3, then K3 from cable needle.

BACK

Using size 6 (4mm) needles, cast on 98 (102: 106: 110: 114) sts.

Row 1 (RS) K2, *P2, K2; rep from * to end.
Row 2 P2, *K2, P2; rep from * to end.
These 2 rows form rib.
Work in rib for 17 rows more, ending with WS facing for next row.
Row 20 (WS) Rib 11 (10: 12: 11: 13), M1, [rib 3, M1] 25 (27: 27: 29: 29) times, rib to end. 124 (130: 134: 140: 144) sts.
Change to size 8 (5mm) needles.
Work in patt as foll:
Row 1 (RS) Knit.
Row 2 K10 (13: 3: 6: 8), P3, K2, P3, *K4, P3, K2, P3; rep from * to last 10 (13: 3: 6: 8) sts, K10 (13: 3: 6: 8).
Row 3 K10 (13: 3: 6: 8), Cr4L, Cr4R, *K4, Cr4L, Cr4R; rep

from * to last 10 (13: 3: 6: 8) sts, K10 (13: 3: 6: 8).

Row 4 K11 (14: 4: 7: 9), P6, K1, *K5, P6, K1; rep from * to last 10 (13: 3: 6: 8) sts, K10 (13: 3: 6: 8).

Row 5 K11 (14: 4: 7: 9), C6B, K1, *K5, C6B, K1; rep from * to last 10 (13: 3: 6: 8) sts, K10 (13: 3: 6: 8).

Row 6 Rep row 4.

Row 7 K10 (13: 3: 6: 8), Cr4R, Cr4L, *K4, Cr4R, Cr4L; rep from * to last 10 (13: 3: 6: 8) sts, K10 (13: 3: 6: 8).

Row 8 Rep row 2.

Rows 9 to 16 Rep rows 1 and 2 four times.

These 16 rows form patt.

Work in patt until Back measures 16½in/42cm from cast-on edge, ending with RS facing for next row.

Shape armholes

Keeping patt correct, bind off 7 (8: 9: 10: 11) sts at beg of next 2 rows. 110 (114: 116: 120: 122) sts.

Dec 1 st at each end of next 5 rows, then on foll 5 (6: 5: 6: 6) alt rows, then on foll 4th row. 88 (90: 94: 96: 98) sts.

Work even until armhole measures 9½ (9¾: 10¼: 10½: 11)in/24 (25: 26: 27: 28)cm, ending with RS facing for next row.

Shape shoulders and back neck

Bind off 8 (9: 9: 9: 9) sts at beg of next 2 rows. 72 (72: 76: 78: 80) sts.

Next row (RS) Bind off 8 (9: 9: 9: 9) sts, patt until there are 13 (12: 13: 13: 13) sts on right needle and turn, leaving rem sts on a holder.

Work each side of neck separately.

Bind off 4 sts at beg of next row.

Bind off rem 9 (8: 9: 9: 9) sts.

With RS facing, rejoin yarn to rem sts, bind off center 30 (30: 32: 34: 36) sts, patt to end.

Complete to match first side, reversing shapings.

FRONT

Work as given for Back until 16 (18: 18: 18: 20) rows less have been worked than on Back to start of shoulder shaping, ending with RS facing for next row.

Shape neck

Next row (RS) Patt 36 (38: 39: 39: 40) sts and turn, leaving rem sts on a holder.

Work each side of neck separately.

Keeping patt correct, bind off 4 sts at beg of next row. 32 (34: 35: 35: 36) sts.

Dec 1 st at neck edge of next 2 rows, then on foll 5 (6: 6: 6: 7) alt rows. 25 (26: 27: 27: 27) sts.

Work 2 rows, ending with RS facing for next row.

Shape shoulder

Bind off 8 (9: 9: 9: 9) sts at beg of next and foll alt row.

Work 1 row.

Bind off rem 9 (8: 9: 9: 9) sts.

With RS facing, slip center 16 (14: 16: 18: 18) sts onto a holder, rejoin yarn to rem sts, patt to end.

Complete to match first side, reversing shapings.

SLEEVES

Using size 6 (4mm) needles, cast on 42 (42: 46: 46: 46) sts.

Work in rib as given for Back for 19 rows, ending with WS facing for next row.

Row 20 (WS) Rib 13 (10: 15: 15: 12), M1, [rib 3, M1] 5 (7: 5: 5: 7) times, rib to end. 48 (50: 52: 52: 54) sts.

Change to size 8 (5mm) needles.

Work in patt as foll:

Row 1 (RS) Knit.

Row 2 K8 (9: 10: 10: 11), P3, K2, P3, [K4, P3, K2, P3] twice, K to end.

Row 3 K8 (9: 10: 10: 11), Cr4L, Cr4R, [K4, Cr4L, Cr4R] twice, K to end.

Row 4 K9 (10: 11: 11: 12), P6, [K6, P6] twice, K to end.

Row 5 [Inc in first st] 0 (1: 1: 1: 1) times, K9 (9: 10: 10: 11), C6B, [K6, C6B] twice, K to last 0 (1: 1: 1: 1) st, [inc in last st] 0 (1: 1: 1: 1) times. 48 (52: 54: 54: 56) sts.

Row 6 K9 (11: 12: 12: 13), P6, [K6, P6] twice, K to end.

Row 7 [Inc in first st] 1 (0: 0: 0: 0) times, K7 (10: 11: 11: 12), Cr4R, Cr4L, [K4, Cr4R, Cr4L] twice, K to last 1 (0: 0: 0: 0) st, [inc in last st] 1 (0: 0: 0: 0) times. 50 (52: 54: 54: 56) sts.

Row 8 K9 (10: 11: 11: 12), P3, K2, P3, [K4, P3, K2, P3] twice, K to end.

Row 9 Knit.

Row 10 Rep row 8.

Row 11 [Inc in first st] 0 (1: 1: 1: 1) times, K to last 0 (1: 1: 1: 1) st, [inc in last st] 0 (1: 1: 1: 1) times. 50 (54: 56: 56: 58) sts.

Row 12 K9 (11: 12: 12: 13), P3, K2, P3, [K4, P3, K2, P3] twice, K to end.

Row 13 Knit.

Row 14 Rep row 12.

Row 15 [Inc in first st] 1 (0: 0: 0: 0) times, K to last 1 (0: 0: 0: 0) st, [inc in last st] 1 (0: 0: 0: 0) times. 52 (54: 56: 56: 58) sts.

Row 16 K10 (11: 12: 12: 13), P3, K2, P3, [K4, P3, K2, P3] twice, K to end.

These 16 rows form patt and start sleeve shaping.

Cont in patt, shaping sides by inc 1 st at each end of 7th (next: next: next: next: next) and every foll 8th (6th: 6th: 6th: 6th) row until there are 74 (58: 66: 82: 88) sts, taking inc sts into garter st.

2ND, 3RD, 4TH, AND 5TH SIZES ONLY

Inc 1 st at each end of every foll 8th row until there are - (78: 82: 86: 90) sts.

ALL SIZES

Work even until Sleeve measures 20½ (20½: 21: 21: 21¼)in/52 (52: 53: 53: 54)cm from cast-on edge, ending with RS facing for next row.

Shape top of sleeve

Keeping patt correct, bind off 7 (8: 9: 10: 11) sts at beg of next 2 rows. 60 (62: 64: 66: 68) sts.

Dec 1 st at each end of next 5 rows, then on foll 5 alt rows, then on every foll 4th row until 32 (34: 36: 38: 40) sts rem.

Work 1 row.

Dec 1 st at each end of next and every foll alt row until 26 sts rem, then on foll 3 rows, ending with RS facing for next row.

Bind off rem 20 sts.

FINISHING

Press lightly on WS following instructions on yarn label.
Sew right shoulder seam.

Neckband

With RS facing and using size 6 (4mm) needles, pick up and knit 22 (23: 22: 25: 25) sts down left side of neck, work across 16 (14: 16: 18: 18) sts on front holder as foll: P0 (0: 0: 1: 1), K2 (1: 2: 2: 2), P2, patt 8 sts, P2, K2 (1: 2: 2: 2), P0 (0: 0: 1: 1), pick up and knit 22 (23: 22: 25: 25) sts up right side of neck, then 40 (40: 40: 44: 44) sts from back. 100 (100: 100: 112: 112) sts.

Row 1 (WS) K2, [P2, K2] 16 (16: 16: 18: 18) times, patt 8 sts, [K2, P2] 6 (6: 6: 7: 7) times, K2.

Row 2 P2, [K2, P2] 6 (6: 6: 7: 7) times, patt 8 sts, [P2, K2] 16 (16: 16: 18: 18) times, P2.

Rep last 2 rows until Neckband measures 3½in/9cm, ending with RS facing for next row.

Bind off in patt.

Sew left shoulder and neckband seam. Sew side and sleeve seams. Sew sleeves into armholes.

STRIPED BEANIE

Martin Storey

SIZE

The finished hat measures 19in/48cm around head.

YARNS

1 x 50g/1¾oz balls of Rowan *Felted Tweed* in each of **MC** (Phantom 153), **A** (Pickle 155), and **B** (Dragon 147)

NEEDLES

Pair of size 3 (3.25mm) knitting needles
Pair of size 5 (3.75mm) knitting needles

GAUGE

23 sts and 32 rows to 4in/10cm measured over St st using size 5 (3.75mm) needles *or size to obtain correct gauge.*

ABBREVIATIONS

See page 133.

HAT

Using size 3 (3.25mm) needles and MC, cast on 110 sts.
Row 1 (RS) K2, *P2, K2; rep from * to end.
Row 2 P2, *K2, P2; rep from * to end.
These 2 rows form rib.
Work in rib for 4 rows more, ending with RS facing for next row.
Change to size 5 (3.75mm) needles.
Starting with a K row and joining in colors as required, work in striped St st as foll:
Rows 1 and 2 Using MC.
Rows 3 and 4 Using A.
Rows 5 and 6 Using MC.
Rows 7 and 8 Using B.
Rows 9 to 16 Rep rows 5 to 8 twice.

These 16 rows form striped St st.
Cont in striped St st until Hat measures 6¼in/16cm from cast-on edge, ending with RS facing for next row.
Shape crown
Keeping stripes correct, work as foll:
Row 1 (RS) K1, [sl 1, K1, psso, K7] 12 times, K1. 98 sts.
Row 2 Purl.
Row 3 K1, [sl 1, K1, psso, K6] 12 times, K1. 86 sts.
Row 4 Purl.
Row 5 K1, [sl 1, K1, psso, K5] 12 times, K1. 74 sts.
Row 6 Purl.
Row 7 K1, [sl 1, K1, psso, K4] 12 times, K1. 62 sts.
Row 8 Purl.
Row 9 K1, [sl 1, K1, psso, K3] 12 times, K1. 50 sts.
Row 10 Purl.
Row 11 K1, [sl 1, K1, psso, K2] 12 times, K1. 38 sts.
Row 12 Purl.
Row 13 K1, [sl 1, K1, psso, K1] 12 times, K1. 26 sts.
Row 14 Purl.
Row 15 K1, [sl 1, K1, psso] 12 times, K1. 14 sts.
Row 16 Purl.
Row 17 K1, [sl 1, K1, psso] 6 times, K1.
Break off yarn and thread through rem 8 sts. Pull up tight and fasten off securely.

FINISHING

Press lightly on WS following instructions on yarn label.
Sew back seam.

SNOWFLAKE JACKET

Martin Storey

To fit chest					
40	42	44	46	48	in
102	107	112	117	122	cm
Finished measurements					
AROUND CHEST					
47½	49½	51½	53½	55½	in
121	126	131	136	141	cm
LENGTH TO BACK NECK					
26	26½	26¾	26¾	27	in
66	67	68	68	69	cm
SLEEVE SEAM					
20½	20½	20¾	20¾	21¼	in
52	52	53	53	54	cm

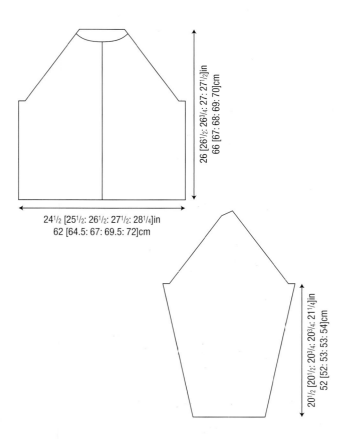

26 [26½: 26¾: 27: 27½]in
66 [67: 68: 69: 70]cm

24½ [25½: 26½: 27½: 28¼]in
62 [64.5: 67: 69.5: 72]cm

20½ [20½: 20¾: 20¾: 21¼]in
52 [52: 53: 53: 54]cm

YARNS

8 (9: 9: 10: 10) x 100g/3½oz balls of Rowan *Scottish Tweed Aran* in **MC** (Midnight 023) and 1 (2: 2: 2: 3) ball in **A** (Lewis Grey 007)

NEEDLES

Pair of size 6 (4mm) knitting needles
Pair of size 8 (5mm) knitting needles

EXTRAS

6 buttons

GAUGE

16 sts and 23 rows to 4in/10cm measured over St st using size 8 (5mm) needles *or size to obtain correct gauge.*

ABBREVIATIONS

See page 133.

SPECIAL NOTE

When working patt from chart, work odd-numbered rows as RS (K) rows, reading them from right to left, and even-numbered rows as WS (P) rows, reading them from left to right. On rows 4 to 8 and rows 36 to 40, strand yarn not in use loosely across WS of work. On rows 12 to 32, use a separate ball of yarn for each block of color, twisting yarns together on WS where they meet to avoid holes forming.

BACK

Using size 6 (4mm) needles and MC, cast on 97 (101: 105: 109: 113) sts.
Row 1 (RS) P0 (1: 0: 0: 1), K2 (3: 0: 2: 3), *P3, K3; rep from * to last 5 (1: 3: 5: 1) sts, P3 (1: 3: 3: 1), K2 (0: 0: 2: 0).
Row 2 K0 (1: 0: 0: 1), P2 (3: 0: 2: 3), *K3, P3; rep from * to last 5 (1: 3: 5: 1) sts, K3 (1: 3: 3: 1), P2 (0: 0: 2: 0).
These 2 rows form rib.

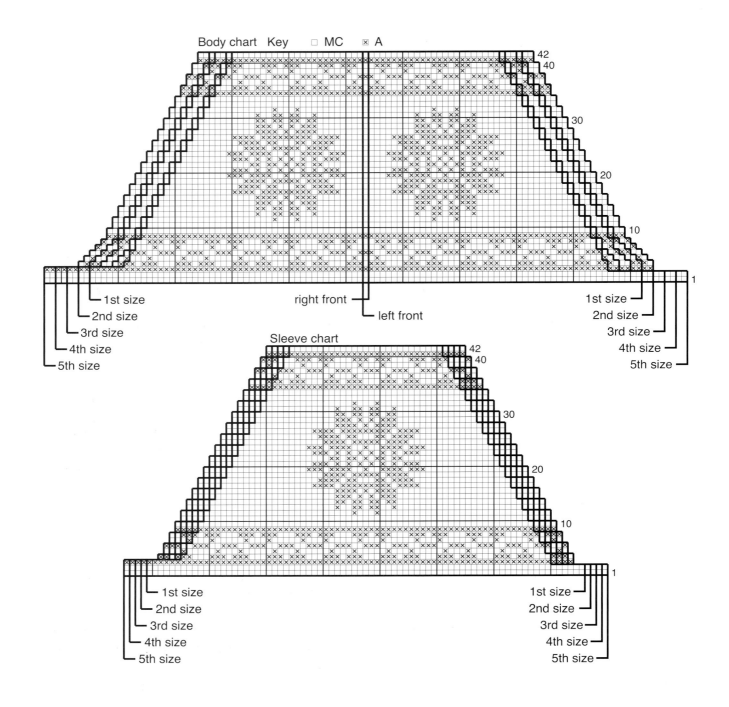

Body chart   Key   ☐ MC   ☒ A

42
40
30
20
10

right front

left front

1

1st size
2nd size
3rd size
4th size
5th size

1st size
2nd size
3rd size
4th size
5th size

Sleeve chart

42
40
30
20
10

1

1st size
2nd size
3rd size
4th size
5th size

1st size
2nd size
3rd size
4th size
5th size

Work in rib for 12 rows more, ending with RS facing for next row.

Change to size 8 (5mm) needles.

Starting with a K row, work in St st until Back measures 14½in/37cm from cast-on edge, ending with RS facing for next row.

Starting and ending rows as indicated, now work in patt from chart for body as foll:

Work 2 rows, ending with RS facing for next row.

Shape raglan armholes

Keeping patt correct, bind off 6 sts at beg of next 2 rows. 85 (89: 93: 97: 101) sts.

Dec 1 st at each end of next 1 (3: 3: 5: 5) rows, then on every foll alt row until 23 (23: 25: 25: 27) sts rem. (**Note:** When all 42 rows of chart have been worked, complete Back in St st using MC only.)

Work 1 row, ending with RS facing for next row.

Bind off.

POCKET LININGS (make 2)

Using size 8 (5mm) needles and MC, cast on 24 sts.

Starting with a K row, work in St st for 32 rows, ending with RS facing for next row.

Break off yarn and leave sts on a holder.

LEFT FRONT

Using size 6 (4mm) needles and MC, cast on 49 (51: 53: 55: 57) sts.

Row 1 (RS) P0 (1: 0: 0: 1), K2 (3: 0: 2: 3), *P3, K3; rep from * to last 5 sts, P3, K2.

Row 2 P2, *K3, P3; rep from * to last 5 (1: 3: 5: 1) sts, K3 (1: 3: 3: 1), P2 (0: 0: 2: 0).

These 2 rows form rib.

Work in rib for 12 rows more, ending with RS facing for next row.

Change to size 8 (5mm) needles.

Starting with a K row, work in St st for 32 rows, ending with RS facing for next row.

Place pocket

Next row (RS) K13 (14: 15: 16: 17), slip next 24 sts onto a holder and, in their place, K across 24 sts of first Pocket Lining, K to end.

Work even until 2 rows less have been worked than on Back to start of raglan armhole shaping, ending with RS facing for next row.

Starting and ending rows as indicated, now work in patt

from chart for body as foll:

Work 2 rows, ending with RS facing for next row.

Shape raglan armhole

Keeping patt correct, bind off 6 sts at beg of next row. 43 (45: 47: 49: 51) sts.

Work 1 row.

Dec 1 st at raglan armhole edge of next 1 (3: 3: 5: 5) rows, then on every foll alt row until 20 (21: 22: 22: 24) sts rem, ending with WS facing for next row. (**Note:** When all 42 rows of chart have been worked, complete Left Front in St st using MC only.)

Shape neck

Bind off 6 (5: 6: 6: 6) sts at beg of next row. 14 (16: 16: 16: 18) sts.

Dec 1 st at each end of next and every foll alt row until 2 sts rem.

Work 1 row, ending with RS facing for next row.

Next row (RS) K2tog and fasten off.

RIGHT FRONT

Using size 6 (4mm) needles and MC, cast on 49 (51: 53: 55: 57) sts.

Row 1 (RS) K2, *P3, K3; rep from * to last 5 (1: 3: 5: 1) sts, P3 (1: 3: 3: 1), K2 (0: 0: 2: 0).

Row 2 K0 (1: 0: 0: 1), P2 (3: 0: 2: 3), *K3, P3; rep from * to last 5 sts, K3, P2.

These 2 rows form rib.

Work in rib for 12 rows more, ending with RS facing for next row.

Change to size 8 (5mm) needles.

Starting with a K row, work in St st for 32 rows, ending with RS facing for next row.

Place pocket

Next row (RS) K12 (13: 14: 15: 16), slip next 24 sts onto a holder and, in their place, K across 24 sts of second Pocket Lining, K to end.

Complete to match Left Front, reversing shapings.

SLEEVES

Using size 6 (4mm) needles and MC, cast on 43 (45: 47: 47: 49) sts.

Row 1 (RS) P2 (0: 0: 0: 0), K3 (0: 1: 1: 2), *P3, K3; rep from * to last 2 (3: 4: 4: 5) sts, P2 (3: 3: 3: 3), K0 (0: 1: 1: 2).

Row 2 K2 (0: 0: 0: 0), P3 (0: 1: 1: 2), *K3, P3; rep from * to last 2 (3: 4: 4: 5) sts, K2 (3: 3: 3: 3), P0 (0: 1: 1: 2).

These 2 rows form rib.

Work in rib for 12 rows more, ending with RS facing for next row.

Change to size 8 (5mm) needles.

Starting with a K row, work in St st, shaping sides by inc 1 st at each end of 3rd and every foll 4th row to 49 (51: 51: 57: 55) sts, then on every foll 6th row until there are 77 (79: 81: 83: 85) sts.

Work even until Sleeve measures 20 (20: 20½: 20½: 20¾)in/51 (51: 52: 52: 53)cm from cast-on edge, ending with RS facing for next row.

Starting and ending rows as indicated, now work in patt from chart for sleeve as foll:

Work 2 rows, ending with RS facing for next row.

Shape raglan

Keeping patt correct, bind off 6 sts at beg of next 2 rows. 65 (67: 69: 71: 73) sts.

Dec 1 st at each end of next and foll alt row until 7 sts rem. (**Note:** When all 42 rows of chart have been worked, complete Sleeve in St st using MC only.)

Work 1 row, ending with RS facing for next row.

LEFT SLEEVE ONLY

Place marker at beg of last row to denote front neck point.

RIGHT SLEEVE ONLY

Place marker at end of last row to denote front neck point.

BOTH SLEEVES

Dec 1 st at marked front neck edge of next 3 rows **and at the same time** dec 1 st at back raglan edge of next and foll alt row. 2 sts.

Next row (WS) P2tog and fasten off.

FINISHING

Press lightly on WS following instructions on yarn label. Sew raglan seams.

Right front band and collar

Using size 6 (4mm) needles and MC, cast on 7 sts.

Work in garter st until Band, when slightly stretched, fits up right front opening edge from cast-on edge to neck shaping, sewing in place as you go along and ending with RS facing for next row.

Shape for collar

Inc 1 st at end (attached edge) of next and every foll alt row until there are 30 sts.

Work even until Collar, unstretched, fits up neck, across top of sleeve, and across to center back neck, sewing in place as you go along.

Bind off.

Mark positions for 6 buttons on this band—first to come in row 5, last to come just below neck shaping, and rem 4 buttons evenly spaced between.

Left front band and collar

Using size 6 (4mm) needles and MC, cast on 7 sts.

Work in garter st until Band, when slightly stretched, fits up left front opening edge from cast-on edge to neck shaping, sewing in place as you go along, ending with RS facing for next row and making 6 buttonholes to correspond with positions marked for buttons as foll:

Buttonhole row (RS) K2, K2tog, yo (to make a buttonhole), K3.

Shape for collar

Inc 1 st at beg (attached edge) of next and every foll alt row until there are 30 sts.

Work even until Collar, unstretched, fits up neck, across top of sleeve, and across to center back neck, sewing in place as you go along.

Bind off.

Sew center back seam of collar by joining bound-off edges.

Pocket borders (both alike)

Slip 24 sts from pocket holder onto size 6 (4mm) needles and rejoin MC with RS facing.

Work in garter st for 5 rows, ending with WS facing for next row.

Bind off knitwise (on WS).

Sew pocket linings in place on inside, then neatly sew down ends of pocket borders. Sew side and sleeve seams. Sew on buttons.

ARGYLL CARDIGAN

Wendy Baker

To fit chest

40	42	44	46	48	in
102	107	112	117	122	cm

Finished measurements

AROUND CHEST

46	48½	50½	52¾	54¾	in
117	123	128	134	139	cm

LENGTH TO BACK NECK

26½	26¾	27	27½	28	in
67	68	69	70	71	cm

SLEEVE SEAM

20½	20½	20¾	20¾	21¼	in
52	52	53	53	54	cm

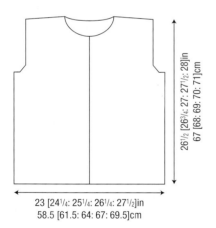

26½ [26¾: 27: 27½: 28]in
67 [68: 69: 70: 71]cm

23 [24¼: 25¼: 26¼: 27½]in
58.5 [61.5: 64: 67: 69.5]cm

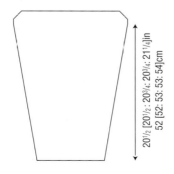

20½ [20½: 20¾: 20¾: 21¼]in
52 [52: 53: 53: 54]cm

YARNS

Rowan *RYC Baby Alpaca DK*:

MC Cheviot 207   14 (15: 16: 17: 17) x 50g/1¾oz balls
A Southdown 208   1 (1: 1: 1: 1) x 50g/1¾oz balls
B Lincoln 209   1 (1: 1: 1: 1) x 50g/1¾oz balls
C Chambray 201   1 (1: 1: 2: 2) x 50g/1¾oz balls

NEEDLES

Pair of size 3 (3.25mm) knitting needles
Pair of size 5 (3.75mm) knitting needles
Pair of size 6 (4mm) knitting needles

EXTRAS

8 buttons

GAUGE

22 sts and 30 rows to 4in/10cm measured over St st using size 6 (4mm) needles *or size to obtain correct gauge.*

ABBREVIATIONS

See page 133.

SPECIAL NOTE

When working patt from chart, use a separate ball of yarn for each block of color, twisting yarns together on WS where they meet to avoid holes forming. Work odd-numbered rows as RS (K) rows, reading them from right to left, and even-numbered rows as WS (P) rows, reading them from left to right.

On Fronts, work chart rows 1 to 84 twice, then complete Fronts by working sts above chart in St st using MC only. On Sleeves, work chart rows 1 to 42 once only, then complete Sleeves by working sts above chart in St st using MC only.

BACK

Using size 5 (3.75mm) needles and B, cast on 129 (135: 141: 147: 153) sts.

Row 1 (RS) K1, *P1, K1; rep from * to end.

Break off B and join in C.

Row 2 Rep row 1.

These 2 rows form seed st.

Work in seed st for 3 rows more, ending with WS facing for next row.

Break off C and join in MC.

Work in seed st for 21 rows more, ending with RS facing for next row.

Change to size 6 (4mm) needles.

Starting with a K row, work in St st until Back measures 17¼in/44cm from cast-on edge, ending with RS facing for next row.

Shape armholes

Bind off 6 sts at beg of next 2 rows. 117 (123: 129: 135: 141) sts.

Next row (RS) K2, sl 1, K1, psso, K to last 4 sts, K2tog, K2.

Working all armhole decreases as set by last row, dec 1 st at each end of 2nd and foll alt row. 111 (117: 123: 129: 135) sts.

Work even until armhole measures 8¼ (8½: 9: 9½: 9¾)in/21 (22: 23: 24: 25)cm, ending with RS facing for next row.

Shape back neck

Next row (RS) K39 (42: 44: 46: 48) and turn, leaving rem sts on a holder.

Work each side of neck separately.

Dec 1 st at neck edge of next 3 rows. 36 (39: 41: 43: 45) sts.

Work 2 rows, ending with RS facing for next row.

Shape shoulder

Bind off 12 (13: 14: 14: 15) sts at beg of next and foll alt row.

Work 1 row.

Bind off rem 12 (13: 13: 15: 15) sts.

With RS facing, rejoin yarn to rem sts, bind off center 33 (33: 35: 37: 39) sts, K to end.

Complete to match first side, reversing shapings.

RIGHT FRONT

Using size 5 (3.75mm) needles and B, cast on 69 (72: 75: 78: 81) sts.

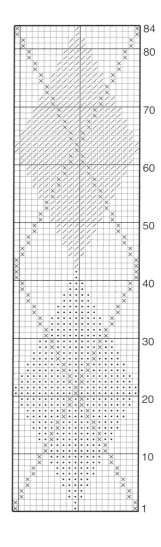

Key
- ☐ MC
- ☑ A
- ☒ B
- ⊡ C

Row 1 (RS) K1 (0: 1: 0: 1), *P1, K1; rep from * to end.

Break off B and join in C.

Row 2 *K1, P1; rep from * to last 1 (0: 1: 0: 1) st, K1 (0: 1: 0: 1).

These 2 rows form seed st.

Work in seed st for 3 rows more, ending with WS facing for next row.

Break off C and join in MC.

Work in seed st for 21 rows more, ending with RS facing for next row.

Change to size 6 (4mm) needles.

Place chart

Next row (RS) Seed st 8 sts, K17 (18: 19: 20: 21), work next 21 sts as row 1 of chart, K to end.

Next row P23 (25: 27: 29: 31), work next 21 sts as row 2 of chart, P to last 8 sts, seed st to end.

These 2 rows set the sts—front opening edge 8 sts still in seed st, and chart worked on a background of St st in MC.

Keeping sts correct throughout and noting that chart rows 1 to 84 are repeated twice only (see Special Note), work even until Right Front matches Back to start of armhole shaping, ending with WS facing for next row.

Shape armhole

Bind off 6 sts at beg of next row. 63 (66: 69: 72: 75) sts.

Working all armhole decreases as set by Back, dec 1 st at armhole edge of next and foll 2 alt rows. 60 (63: 66: 69: 72) sts.

Work even until 18 (20: 20: 20: 22) rows less have been worked than on Back to start of shoulder shaping, ending with RS facing for next row.

Shape neck

Next row (RS) Patt 14 (13: 14: 15: 15) sts and slip these sts onto a holder, patt to end. 46 (50: 52: 54: 57) sts.

Dec 1 st at neck edge of next 8 rows, then on 2 (3: 3: 3: 4) alt rows. 36 (39: 41: 43: 45) sts.

Work 6 rows, ending with WS facing for next row.

Shape shoulder

Bind off 12 (13: 14: 14: 15) sts at beg of next and foll alt row.

Work 1 row.

Bind off rem 12 (13: 13: 15: 15) sts.

Mark positions for 7 buttons along front opening edge—first to come in row 15, last to come just below start of neck shaping, and rem 5 buttons evenly spaced between.

LEFT FRONT

Using size 5 (3.75mm) needles and B, cast on 69 (72: 75: 78: 81) sts.

Row 1 (RS) *K1, P1; rep from * to last 1 (0: 1: 0: 1) st, K1 (0: 1: 0: 1).

Break off B and join in C.

Row 2 K1 (0: 1: 0: 1), *P1, K1; rep from * to end.

These 2 rows form seed st.

Work in seed st for 3 rows more, ending with WS facing for next row.

Break off C and join in MC.

Work in seed st for 9 rows more, ending with RS facing for next row.

Row 15 (buttonhole row) (RS) Patt to last 5 sts, bind off 2 sts (to make a buttonhole—cast on 2 sts over these

bound-off sts on next row), seed st to end.

Working 6 more buttonholes in this way to correspond with positions marked for buttons on Right Front and noting that no more references will be made to buttonholes, cont as foll:

Work in seed st for 11 rows more, ending with RS facing for next row.

Change to size 6 (4mm) needles.

Place chart

Next row (RS) K23 (25: 27: 29: 31), work next 21 sts as row 1 of chart, K to last 8 sts, seed st to end.

Next row Seed st 8 sts, P17 (18: 19: 20: 21), work next 21 sts as row 2 of chart, P to end.

These 2 rows set the sts—front opening edge 8 sts still in seed st, and chart worked on a background of St st in MC.

Complete to match Right Front, reversing shapings.

SLEEVES

Using size 5 (3.75mm) needles and B, cast on 53 (55: 57: 57: 59) sts.

Work in seed st as given for Back for 1 row.

Break off B and join in C.

Work in seed st for 4 rows more, ending with WS facing for next row.

Break off C and join in MC.

Work in seed st for 21 rows more, ending with RS facing for next row.

Change to size 6 (4mm) needles.

Place chart

Next row (RS) K16 (17: 18: 18: 19), work next 21 sts as row 1 of chart, K to end.

Next row P16 (17: 18: 18: 19), work next 21 sts as row 2 of chart, P to end.

These 2 rows set the sts—chart worked on a background of St st in MC.

Keeping sts correct throughout and noting that chart rows 1 to 42 are repeated once only (see Special Note), work as set, shaping sides by inc 1 st at each end of next and every foll 4th row until there are 95 (103: 107: 119: 123) sts.

1ST, 2ND, AND 3RD SIZES

Inc 1 st at each end of every foll 6th row until there are 107 (111: 115: -: -) sts.

ALL SIZES

Work even until Sleeve measures 20½ (20½: 20¾: 20¾: 21¼)in/52 (52: 53: 53: 54)cm from cast-on edge, ending with RS facing for next row.

Shape top of sleeve

Place markers at both ends of last row to denote top of sleeve seam.

Work 8 rows, ending with RS facing for next row.

Working all decreases in same way as armhole decreases, dec 1 st at each end of next and foll 2 alt rows. 101 (105: 109: 113: 117) sts.

Work 1 row.

Bind off 8 sts at beg of next 10 rows, ending with RS facing for next row.

Bind off rem 21 (25: 29: 33: 37) sts.

FINISHING

Press lightly on WS following instructions on yarn label. Sew shoulder seams.

Collar

With RS facing, using size 3 (3.25mm) needles and MC, slip 14 (13: 14: 15: 15) sts from right front holder onto right needle, rejoin yarn and pick up and knit 16 (18: 18: 18: 20) sts up right side of neck, 47 (47: 49: 51: 53) sts from back, and 16 (18: 18: 18: 20) sts down left side of neck, then patt across 14 (13: 14: 15: 15) sts from left front holder. 107 (109: 113: 117: 123) sts.

Work in seed st as set by front opening edge sts until Collar measures 3½in/9cm from pick-up row, ending with RS facing for next row.

Next row (RS) Seed st to last 5 sts, bind off 2 sts (to make 8th buttonhole—cast on 2 sts over these bound-off sts on next row), seed st to end.

Work 1 row more, ending with RS facing for next row.

Break off MC and join in C.

Work in seed st for 4 rows.

Break off C and join in B.

Work in seed st for 1 row more, ending with WS facing for next row.

Bind off in seed st (on WS).

Sew sleeves into armholes, matching center of sleeve bound-off edge to shoulder seam and sleeve markers to top of side seams. Sew side and sleeve seams. Sew on buttons.

STRIPED
SWEATER

Wendy Baker

To fit chest

40	42	44	46	48	in
102	107	112	117	122	cm

Finished measurements

AROUND CHEST

46	48½	50½	52¾	54¾	in
117	123	128	134	139	cm

LENGTH TO BACK NECK

26½	26¾	27½	28	28¾	in
67	68	70	71	73	cm

SLEEVE SEAM

20	20	20½	20½	20¾	in
51	51	52	52	53	cm

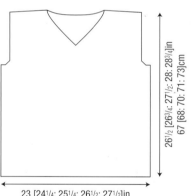

26½ [26¾: 27½: 28: 28¾]in
67 [68: 70: 71: 73]cm

23 [24¼: 25¼: 26½: 27½]in
58.5 [61.5: 64: 67: 69.5]cm

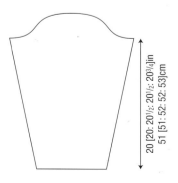

20 [20: 20½: 20½: 20¾]in
51 [51: 52: 52: 53]cm

YARNS

Rowan *Scottish Tweed DK*:

MC Lewis Grey 007   5 (5: 6: 6: 6) x 50g/1¾oz balls
A Grey Mist 001   2 (2: 3: 3: 3) x 50g/1¾oz balls
B Sunset 011   2 (2: 2: 3: 3) x 50g/1¾oz balls
C Midnight 023   1 (1: 1: 2: 2) x 50g/1¾oz balls
D Stormy Grey 004   5 (5: 6: 6: 6) x 50g/1¾oz balls

NEEDLES

Pair of size 5 (3.75mm) knitting needles
Pair of size 6 (4mm) knitting needles

GAUGE

22 sts and 30 rows to 4in/10cm measured over St st using size 6 (4mm) needles *or size to obtain correct gauge.*

ABBREVIATIONS

See page 133.

STRIPE SEQUENCE

Rows 1 and 2 Using A.
Rows 3 and 4 Using B.
Rows 5 and 6 Using C.
Rows 7 to 20 Using D.
(**Note:** For Sleeves only, repeat rows 1 to 20 once more before continuing with rows 21 onward.)
Rows 21 to 28 Using A.
Rows 29 to 32 Using MC.
Rows 33 to 40 Using B.
Rows 41 to 46 Using MC.
Rows 47 to 56 Using D.
Rows 57 and 58 Using C.
Rows 59 and 60 Using D.
Rows 61 to 66 Using A.
Rows 67 to 72 Using C.
Rows 73 to 80 Using D.
Rows 81 to 94 Using MC.
Rows 95 and 96 Using A.
Rows 97 and 98 Using D.
Rows 99 and 100 Using B.
Rows 101 and 102 Using D.
Rows 103 and 104 Using C.
Rows 105 to 116 Using D.
Rows 117 to 124 Using MC.
Rows 125 and 126 Using B.

Rows 127 to 130 Using A.
Rows 131 to 144 Using MC.
Rows 145 onward Using D.

BACK

Using size 5 (3.75mm) needles and MC, cast on 129 (135: 141: 147: 153) sts.
Row 1 (WS) K2 (1: 4: 3: 2), P5, *K3, P5; rep from * to last 2 (1: 4: 3: 2) sts, K2 (1: 4: 3: 2).
Row 2 P2 (1: 4: 3: 2), slip next 5 sts purlwise with yarn at front (RS) of work, *P3, slip next 5 sts purlwise with yarn at front (RS) of work; rep from * to last 2 (1: 4: 3: 2) sts, P2 (1: 4: 3: 2).
Row 3 Rep row 1.
Row 4 K4 (3: 6: 5: 4), K next st lifting up strand of yarn of row 2 directly below this st and enclosing this strand in st, *K7, K next st lifting up strand of yarn of row 2 directly below this st and enclosing this strand in st; rep from * to last 4 (3: 6: 5: 4) sts, K4 (3: 6: 5: 4).
These 4 rows form fancy rib.
Work in fancy rib for 17 rows more, ending with RS facing for next row.
Change to size 6 (4mm) needles.
Joining in and breaking off colors as required, starting with a K row and row 1, work in St st in stripe sequence (as given above) until Back measures 17¼ (17¼: 17¾: 17¾: 18)in/44 (44: 45: 45: 46)cm, ending with RS facing for next row.

Shape armholes

Keeping stripes correct, bind off 6 sts at beg of next 2 rows. 117 (123: 129: 135: 141) sts.
Next row (RS) K2, sl 1, K1, psso, K to last 4 sts, K2tog, K2.
Working all armhole decreases as set by last row, dec 1 st at each end of 2nd and foll 4 alt rows. 105 (111: 117: 123: 129) sts.**
Work even until armhole measures 8¼ (8½: 9: 9½: 9¾)in/21 (22: 23: 24: 25)cm, ending with RS facing for next row.

Shape back neck

Next row (RS) K34 (37: 39: 41: 43) and turn, leaving rem sts on a holder.
Work each side of neck separately.
Keeping stripes correct, dec 1 st at neck edge of next 4 rows. 30 (33: 35: 37: 39) sts.
Work 1 row, ending with RS facing for next row.

Shape shoulder

Bind off 10 (11: 12: 12: 13) sts at beg of next and foll alt row.

Work 1 row.

Bind off rem 10 (11: 11: 13: 13) sts.

With RS facing, rejoin appropriate yarn to rem sts, bind off center 37 (37: 39: 41: 43) sts, K to end.

Complete to match first side, reversing shapings.

FRONT

Work as given for Back to **.

Work 9 rows, ending with RS facing for next row.

Divide for neck

Next row (RS) K52 (55: 58: 61: 64) and turn, leaving rem sts on a holder.

Work each side of neck separately.

Keeping stripes correct, dec 1 st at neck edge of next (next: 2nd: 2nd: 2nd) and foll 3 (1: 0: 0: 0) rows, then on every foll alt row until 30 (33: 35: 37: 39) sts rem.

Work even until Front matches Back to start of shoulder shaping, ending with RS facing for next row.

Shape shoulder

Bind off 10 (11: 12: 12: 13) sts at beg of next and foll alt row.

Work 1 row.

Bind off rem 10 (11: 11: 13: 13) sts.

With RS facing, slip center st onto a holder, rejoin appropriate yarn to rem sts, K to end.

Complete to match first side, reversing shapings.

SLEEVES

Using size 5 (3.75mm) needles and MC, cast on 57 (59: 61: 61: 63) sts.

Row 1 (WS) K2 (3: 4: 4: 5), P5, *K3, P5; rep from * to last 2 (3: 4: 4: 5) sts, K2 (3: 4: 4: 5).

Row 2 P2 (3: 4: 4: 5), slip next 5 sts purlwise with yarn at front (RS) of work, *P3, slip next 5 sts purlwise with yarn at front (RS) of work; rep from * to last 2 (3: 4: 4: 5) sts, P2 (3: 4: 4: 5).

Row 3 Rep row 1.

Row 4 K4 (5: 6: 6: 7), K next st lifting up strand of yarn of row 2 directly below this st and enclosing this strand in st, *K7, K next st lifting up strand of yarn of row 2 directly below this st and enclosing this strand in st; rep from * to last 4 (5: 6: 6: 7) sts, K4 (5: 6: 6: 7).

These 4 rows form fancy rib.

Work in fancy rib for 17 rows more, ending with RS facing for next row.

Change to size 6 (4mm) needles.

Joining in and breaking off colors as required, starting with a K row and row 1, work in St st in stripe sequence (as given above and noting that rows 1 to 20 are worked twice), shaping sides by inc 1 st at each end of 3rd and every foll 4th row to 87 (95: 99: 111: 117) sts, then on every foll 6th row until there are 107 (111: 115: 119: 123) sts.

Work even until Sleeve measures approximately 20 (20: 20½: 20½: 20¾)in/51 (51: 52: 52: 53)cm from cast-on edge, ending after same stripe row as on Back to start of armhole shaping and with RS facing for next row.

Shape top of sleeve

Keeping stripes correct, bind off 6 sts at beg of next 2 rows. 95 (99: 103: 107: 111) sts.

Working decreases in same way as for armhole decreases, dec 1 st at each end of next and foll 5 alt rows. 83 (87: 91: 95: 99) sts.

Work 1 row, ending with RS facing for next row.

Bind off 4 sts at beg of next 16 rows.

Bind off rem 19 (23: 27: 31: 35) sts.

FINISHING

Press lightly on WS following instructions on yarn label.

Sew right shoulder seam.

Neckband

With RS facing, using size 5 (3.75mm) needles and MC, pick up and knit 39 (41: 43: 45: 47) sts down left side of neck, K st left on holder at base of V and mark this st with a colored thread, pick up and knit 39 (41: 43: 45: 47) sts up right side of neck, then 53 (53: 55: 57: 59) sts from back. 132 (136: 142: 148: 154) sts.

Row 1 (WS) Knit.

Row 2 K to within 2 sts of marked st, K2tog, K marked st, sl 1, K1, psso, K to end.

Rep last 2 rows 7 times more, then first of these 2 rows again, ending with RS facing for next row. 116 (120: 126: 132: 138) sts.

Bind off knitwise, still decreasing either side of marked st as before.

Sew left shoulder and neckband seam. Sew side and sleeve seams. Sew sleeves into armholes.

FAIR ISLE VEST

Wendy Baker

To fit chest

40	42	44	46	48	in
102	107	112	117	122	cm

Finished measurements

AROUND CHEST

38½	40½	43	45	46¾	in
98	103	109	114	119	cm

LENGTH TO BACK NECK

22½	22¾	23¼	23½	24	in
57	58	59	60	61	cm

YARNS

Rowan *Scottish Tweed 4 ply*:

MC Storm Grey 004   7 (8: 8: 9: 9) x 25g/⅞oz balls
A Claret 013   1 (1: 2: 2: 2) x 25g/⅞oz balls
B Celtic Mix 022   1 (1: 1: 2: 2) x 25g/⅞oz balls
C Lewis Grey 007   2 (2: 2: 3: 3) x 25g/⅞oz balls
D Apple 015   1 (1: 1: 2: 2) x 25g/⅞oz balls

NEEDLES

Pair of size 2 (3mm) knitting needles
Pair of size 3 (3.25mm) knitting needles

EXTRAS

6 buttons

GAUGE

30 sts and 38 rows to 4in/10cm measured over patt using size 3 (3.25mm) needles *or size to obtain correct gauge*.

ABBREVIATIONS

See page 133.

SPECIAL NOTE

When working patt from chart, strand yarn not in use loosely across WS of work. Work odd-numbered rows as

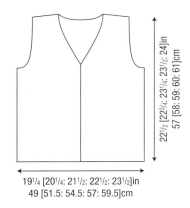

19¼ [20¼: 21½: 22½: 23½]in
49 [51.5: 54.5: 57: 59.5]cm

22½ [22¾: 23¼: 23½: 24]in
57 [58: 59: 60: 61]cm

RS (K) rows, reading them from right to left, and even-numbered rows as WS (P) rows, reading them from left to right.

BACK

Using size 2 (3mm) needles and C, cast on 147 (155: 163: 171: 179) sts.
Break off C and join in A.
Row 1 (RS) [K1 tbl] 0 (0: 0: 1: 0) times, P0 (0: 0: 1: 1), K2 (1: 0: 2: 2), *P1, K1 tbl, P1, K2; rep from * to last 0 (4: 3: 2: 1) sts, P0 (1: 1: 1: 1), [K1 tbl] 0 (1: 1: 1: 0) times, P0 (1: 1: 0: 0), K0 (1: 0: 0: 0).
Row 2 P0 (0: 0: 1: 0), K0 (0: 0: 1: 1), P2 (1: 0: 2: 2), *K1, P1, K1, P2; rep from * to last 0 (4: 3: 2: 1) sts, K0 (1: 1: 1: 1), P0 (1: 1: 1: 0), K0 (1: 0: 0: 0), P0 (1: 0: 0: 0).
Row 3 [K1 tbl] 0 (0: 0: 1: 0) times, P2 (1: 0: 3: 3), *P1, K1 tbl, P3; rep from * to last 0 (4: 3: 2: 1) sts, P0 (1: 1: 1: 1), [K1 tbl] 0 (1: 1: 1: 0) times, P0 (2: 1: 0: 0).
Row 4 P0 (0: 0: 1: 0), K2 (1: 0: 3: 3), *K1, P1, K3; rep from * to last 0 (4: 3: 2: 1) sts, K0 (1: 1: 1: 1), P0 (1: 1: 1: 0), K0 (2: 1: 0: 0).
These 4 rows form fancy rib.
Joining in and breaking off colors as required, work in striped fancy rib as foll:

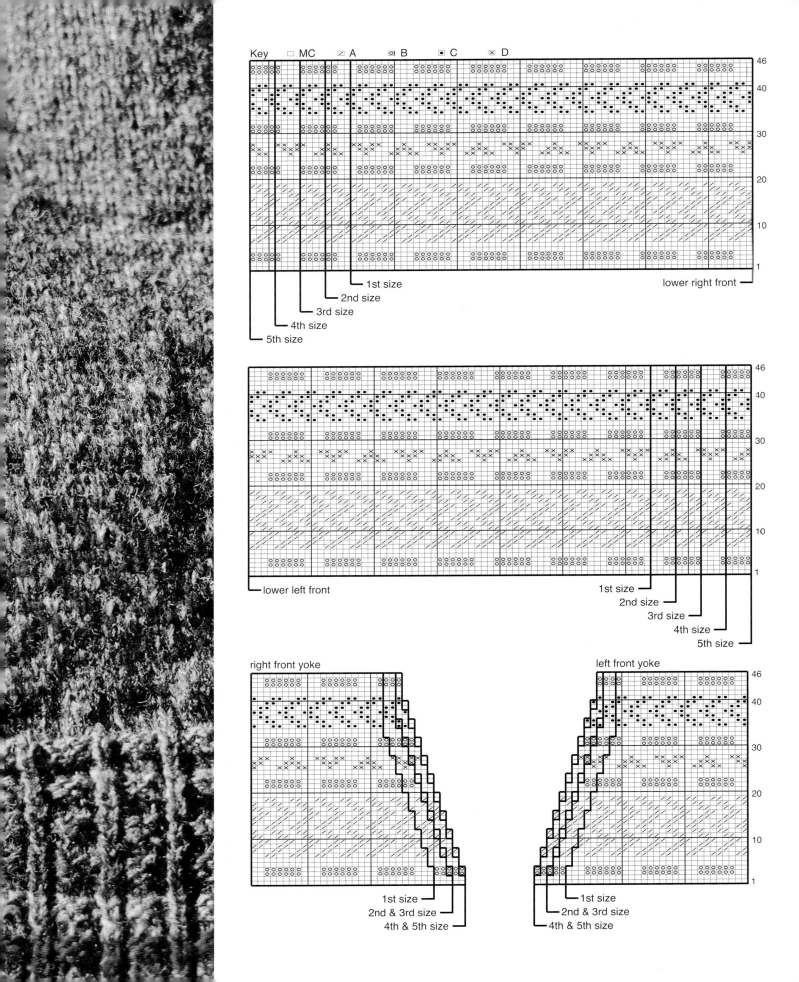

Key □ MC ◪ A ⊡ B ● C ⊠ D

46
40
30
20
10
1

1st size
2nd size
3rd size
4th size
5th size

lower right front

46
40
30
20
10
1

lower left front

1st size
2nd size
3rd size
4th size
5th size

right front yoke

left front yoke

46
40
30
20
10
1

1st size
2nd & 3rd size
4th & 5th size

1st size
2nd & 3rd size
4th & 5th size

Using MC, work 4 rows.

Using B, work 4 rows.

Using C, work 4 rows.

Using MC, work 4 rows.

Using D, work 4 rows, ending with RS facing for next row.

Break off contrasting colours and cont using MC only.

Change to size 3 (3.25mm) needles.

Work in fancy rib until Back measures 13¾in/35cm from cast-on edge, ending with RS facing for next row.

Joining in separate balls of yarn and twisting colors together on WS where they meet to avoid holes forming, cont as foll:

Next row (RS) Using C K12 (13: 14: 15: 16), using MC patt to last 12 (13: 14: 15: 16) sts, using C K12 (13: 14: 15: 16).

Next row Using C K12 (13: 14: 15: 16), using MC patt to last 12 (13: 14: 15: 16) sts, using C K12 (13: 14: 15: 16).

These 2 rows set the sts—underarm and armhole edge sts now in garter st using C and all other sts still in patt using MC.

Keeping sts correct as set, work 6 rows more, ending with RS facing for next row.

Shape armholes

Keeping patt correct, bind off 6 (7: 8: 9: 10) sts at beg of next 2 rows. 135 (141: 147: 153: 159) sts.

Next row (RS) Using C K5, sl 1, K1, psso, using MC patt to last 7 sts, using C K2tog, K5.

Next row Using C K6, using MC patt to last 6 sts, using C K6.

Rep last 2 rows 13 (14: 15: 16: 17) times more. 107 (111: 115: 119: 123) sts.

Keeping sts correct as set, work even until armhole measures 7½ (7¾: 8¼: 8½: 9)in/19 (20: 21: 22: 23)cm, ending with RS facing for next row.

Shape back neck and shoulders

Next row (RS) Patt 35 (37: 37: 38: 38) sts and turn, leaving rem sts on a holder.

Work each side of neck separately.

Dec 1 st at neck edge of next 5 rows **and at the same time** bind off 10 (11: 11: 11: 11) sts at beg of 2nd and foll alt row.

Bind off rem 10 (10: 10: 11: 11) sts.

With RS facing, rejoin yarns to rem sts, bind off center 37 (37: 41: 43: 47) sts, patt to end.

Complete to match first side, reversing shapings.

RIGHT FRONT

Using size 2 (3mm) needles and C, cast on 72 (76: 80: 84: 88) sts.

Join in A.

Twisting yarns together on WS where they meet to avoid holes forming, cont as foll:

Row 1 (RS) Using C K8, using A K1 tbl, P1, K2, *P1, K1 tbl, P1, K2; rep from * to last 0 (4: 3: 2: 1) sts, P0 (1: 1: 1: 1), [K1 tbl] 0 (1: 1: 1: 0) times, P0 (1: 1: 0: 0), K0 (1: 0: 0: 0).

Row 2 Using A P0 (0: 0: 1: 0), K0 (0: 0: 1: 1), P2 (1: 0: 2: 2), *K1, P1, K1, P2; rep from * to last 10 sts, K1, P1, using C K8.

Row 3 Using C K8, using A K1 tbl, P3, *P1, K1 tbl, P3; rep from * to last 0 (4: 3: 2: 1) sts, P0 (1: 1: 1: 1), [K1 tbl] 0 (1: 1: 1: 0) times, P0 (2: 1: 0: 0).

Row 4 Using A P0 (0: 0: 1: 0), K2 (1: 0: 3: 3), *K1, P1, K3; rep from * to last 10 sts, K1, P1, using C K8.

These 4 rows set the sts—front opening edge 8 sts in garter st using C and all other sts in fancy rib as for Back.

Joining in and breaking off colors as required, work in striped fancy rib as foll:

Rows 5 to 8 Rep rows 1 to 4 but using MC in place of A.

Rows 9 to 12 Rep rows 1 to 4 but using B in place of A.

Rows 13 to 16 Rep rows 1 to 4 but using C in place of A.

Rows 17 to 20 Rep rows 1 to 4 but using MC in place of A.

Rows 21 to 24 Rep rows 1 to 4 but using D in place of A.

Change to size 3 (3.25mm) needles.

Starting and ending rows as indicated and joining in and breaking off colors as required, now work in patt from chart for Lower Right Front as foll:

Row 1 (RS) Using C K8, work last 64 (68: 72: 76: 80) sts as row 1 of chart.

Row 2 Work first 64 (68: 72: 76: 80) sts as row 2 of chart, using C K8.

These 2 rows set the sts—front opening edge 8 sts still in garter st using C and all other sts now in Fair Isle patt from chart.

Work even as set until all 46 rows of chart have been completed, ending with RS facing for next row.

Next row (RS) Using C K8, using MC K to end.

Next row Using MC P to last 8 sts, using C K8.

Rep last 2 rows until Right Front measures 13¾in/35cm from cast-on edge, ending with RS facing for next row.

Joining in separate balls of yarn and twisting colors together on WS where they meet to avoid holes forming, cont as foll:

Next row (RS) Using C K8, using MC K to last 12 (13: 14: 15: 16) sts, using C K12 (13: 14: 15: 16).

Next row Using C K12 (13: 14: 15: 16), using MC P to last 8 sts, using C K8.

These 2 rows set the sts—underarm, armhole, and front opening edge sts now in garter st using C and all other sts still in St st using MC.

Keeping sts correct as set, work 7 rows more, ending with WS facing for next row.

Shape armhole

Keeping patt correct, bind off 6 (7: 8: 9: 10) sts at beg of next row. 66 (69: 72: 75: 78) sts.

Shape front slope

Next row (RS) Using C K7, sl 1, K1, psso (for front slope decrease), using MC K to last 7 sts, using C K2tog (for armhole decrease), K5. 64 (67: 70: 73: 76) sts.

Next row Using C K6, using MC patt to last 8 sts, using C K8.

Working all decreases as now set and keeping sts correct, dec 1 st at armhole edge of next and foll 12 (13: 14: 15: 16) alt rows **and at the same time** dec 1 st at front slope edge of next (3rd: next: next: next) and foll 1 (0: 1: 1: 3) alt rows, then on every foll 4th row. 44 (46: 47: 48: 49) sts.

Work 1 row, ending with RS facing for next row.

Starting and ending rows as indicated, now work in patt from chart for Right Front Yoke as foll:

Next row (RS) Using C K7 (8: 7: 8: 7), [sl 1, K1, psso] 1 (0: 1: 0: 1) times, work next 29 (32: 32: 34: 34) sts as row 1 of chart, using C K6. 43 (46: 46: 48: 48) sts.

Next row Using C K6, work next 29 (32: 32: 34: 34) sts as row 2 of chart, using C K8.

These 2 rows set the sts—armhole and front border sts still in garter st using C and all other sts now worked from chart.

Keeping sts and chart correct (and working sts above chart in St st using MC once all 46 rows have been completed), cont as foll:

Dec 1 st at front slope edge of 3rd (next: 3rd: next: 3rd) and every foll 4th row until 35 (37: 37: 38: 38) sts rem.

Work even until Right Front matches Back to start of shoulder shaping, ending with WS facing for next row.

Shape shoulder

Bind off 9 (10: 10: 10: 10) sts at beg of next and foll alt row, then 9 (9: 9: 10: 10) sts at beg of foll alt row. 8 sts.

Work in garter st using C on these 8 sts only until this back neckband extension measures 3 (3: 3¼: 3½: 3¾)in8 / (8: 8.5: 9: 9.5)cm, ending with RS facing for next row. Bind off.

Mark positions for 6 buttons along right front opening edge—first to come in row 5, last to come ⅜in/1cm below start of front slope shaping and rem 4 buttons evenly spaced between.

LEFT FRONT

Using size 2 (3mm) needles and C, cast on 72 (76: 80: 84: 88) sts.

Join in A.

Twisting yarns together on WS where they meet to avoid holes forming, cont as foll:

Row 1 (RS) Using A [K1 tbl] 0 (0: 0: 1: 0) times, P0 (0: 0: 1: 1), K2 (1: 0: 2: 2), *P1, K1 tbl, P1, K2; rep from * to last 10 sts, P1, K1 tbl, using C K8.

Row 2 Using C K8, using A P1, K1, P2, *K1, P1, K1, P2; rep from * to last 0 (4: 3: 2: 1) sts, K0 (1: 1: 1: 1), P0 (1: 1: 1: 0), K0 (1: 1: 0: 0), P0 (1: 0: 0: 0).

Row 3 Using A [K1 tbl] 0 (0: 0: 1: 0) times, P2 (1: 0: 3: 3), *P1, K1 tbl, P3; rep from * to last 10 sts, P1, K1 tbl, using C K8.

Row 4 Using C K8, using A P1, K3, *K1, P1, K3; rep from * to last 0 (4: 3: 2: 1) sts, K0 (1: 1: 1: 1), P0 (1: 1: 1: 0), K0 (2: 1: 0: 0).

These 4 rows set the sts—front opening edge 8 sts in garter st using C and all other sts in fancy rib as for Back. Joining in and breaking off colors as required, work in striped fancy rib as foll:

Row 5 (RS) Using MC [K1 tbl] 0 (0: 0: 1: 0) times, P0 (0: 0: 1: 1), K2 (1: 0: 2: 2), *P1, K1 tbl, P1, K2; rep from * to last 10 sts, P1, K1 tbl, using C K2, bind off 2 sts (to make a buttonhole—cast on 2 sts over these bound-off sts on next row), K to end.

Working 5 buttonholes more in this way to correspond with positions marked for buttons on Right Front and nothing that buttonholes will not be mentioned again, cont as foll:

Rows 6 to 8 Rep rows 2 to 4 but using MC in place of A.

Rows 9 to 12 Rep rows 1 to 4 but using B in place of A.

Rows 13 to 16 Rep rows 1 to 4 but using C in place of A.

Rows 17 to 20 Rep rows 1 to 4 but using MC in place of A.

Rows 21 to 24 Rep rows 1 to 4 but using D in place of A.

Change to size 3 (3.25mm) needles.

Starting and ending rows as indicated and joining in and

breaking off colors as required, now work in patt from chart for Lower Left Front as foll:

Row 1 (RS) Work first 64 (68: 72: 76: 80) sts as row 1 of chart, using C K8.

Row 2 Using C K8, work last 64 (68: 72: 76: 80) sts as row 2 of chart.

These 2 rows set the sts—front opening edge 8 sts still in garter st using C and all other sts now in Fair Isle patt from chart.

Work even as set until all 46 rows of chart have been completed, ending with RS facing for next row.

Next row (RS) Using MC K to last 8 sts, using C K8.

Next row Using C K8, using MC P to end.

Rep last 2 rows until Left Front measures 13¾in/35cm from cast-on edge, ending with RS facing for next row.

Joining in separate balls of yarn and twisting colors together on WS where they meet to avoid holes forming, cont as foll:

Next row (RS) Using C K12 (13: 14: 15: 16), using MC K to last 8 sts, using C K8.

Next row Using C K8, using MC P to last 12 (13: 14: 15: 16) sts, using C K12 (13: 14: 15: 16).

These 2 rows set the sts—underarm, armhole, and front opening edge sts now in garter st using C and all other sts still in St st using MC.

Keeping sts correct as set, work 6 rows more, ending with RS facing for next row.

Shape armhole

Keeping patt correct, bind off 6 (7: 8: 9: 10) sts at beg of next row. 66 (69: 72: 75: 78) sts.

Work 1 row.

Shape front slope

Next row (RS) Using C K5, sl 1, K1, psso (for armhole decrease), using MC K to last 9 sts, using C K2tog (for front slope decrease), K7. 64 (67: 70: 73: 76) sts.

Next row Using C K8, using MC patt to last 6 sts, using C K6.

Working all decreases as now set and keeping sts correct, complete to match Right Front, reversing shapings.

FINISHING

Press lightly on WS following instructions on yarn label. Sew shoulder seams. Join bound-off edges of back neckband extensions, then sew one edge to back neck. Sew side seams. Sew on buttons.

CRICKET SWEATER

Wendy Baker

To fit chest

40	42	44	46	48	in
102	107	112	117	122	cm

Finished measurements

AROUND CHEST

48	50	52¼	54¼	56½	in
122	127	133	138	144	cm

LENGTH TO BACK NECK

26	26½	26¾	27	27½	in
66	67	68	69	70	cm

SLEEVE SEAM

20½	20½	20¾	20¾	21¼	in
52	52	53	53	54	cm

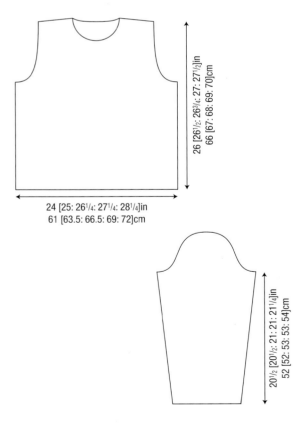

26 [26½: 26¾: 27: 27½]in
66 [67: 68: 69: 70]cm

24 [25: 26¼: 27¼: 28¼]in
61 [63.5: 66.5: 69: 72]cm

20½ [20½: 21: 21: 21¼]in
52 [52: 53: 53: 54]cm

YARNS

17 (18: 19: 20: 20) x 50g/1¾oz balls of Rowan *RYC Baby Alpaca DK* in **MC** (Southdown 208) and 1 (1: 1: 2: 2) balls in **A** (Lincoln 209)

NEEDLES

Pair of size 3 (3.25mm) knitting needles
Pair of size 6 (4mm) knitting needles
Size 3 (3.25mm) circular knitting needle

GAUGE

22 sts and 30 rows to 4in/10cm measured over St st using size 6 (4mm) needles *or size to obtain correct gauge.* Cable panel (109 sts) measures 15¾in/40cm.

ABBREVIATIONS

See page 133.

SPECIAL ABBREVIATIONS

Cr3R = slip next st onto cable needle and leave at back of work, K2, then P1 from cable needle; **Cr3L** = slip next 2 sts onto cable needle and leave at front of work, P1, then K2 from cable needle; **Cr4R** = slip next st onto cable needle and leave at back of work, K1 tbl, P1, K1 tbl, then P1 from cable needle; **Cr4L** = slip next 3 sts onto cable needle and leave at front of work, P1, then K1 tbl, P1, K1 tbl from cable needle; **C5B** = slip next 3 sts onto cable needle and leave at back of work, K2, then P1, K2 from cable needle; **C7B** = slip next 4 sts onto cable needle and leave at back of work, K1 tbl, P1, K1 tbl, then [P1, K1 tbl] twice from cable needle.

BACK

Using size 3 (3.25mm) needles and MC, cast on 128 (134: 140: 146: 152) sts.
Row 1 (RS) P1 (0: 0: 0: 1), K2 (2: 1: 0: 2), *P2, K2; rep from * to last 1 (0: 3: 2: 1) sts, P1 (0: 2: 2: 1), K0 (0: 1: 0: 0).

Row 2 K1 (0: 0: 0: 1), P2 (2: 1: 0: 2), *K2, P2; rep from * to last 1 (0: 3: 2: 1) sts, K1 (0: 2: 2: 1), P0 (0: 1: 0: 0).

These 2 rows form rib.

***Work in rib for 10 rows more, ending with RS facing for next row.

Join in A.

Using A, work in rib for 6 rows.

Using MC, work in rib for 6 rows.

Using A, work in rib for 5 rows, ending with WS facing for next row.***

Row 30 (WS) Using A, rib 31 (34: 37: 40: 43), *[M1, rib 1] twice, M1, rib 4, [M1, rib 3] twice, M1, rib 4; rep from * 3 times more, [M1, rib 1] twice, M1, rib to end. 155 (161: 167: 173: 179) sts.

Break off A and cont using MC only.

Change to size 6 (4mm) needles.

Starting and ending rows as indicated and repeating the 24 row patt repeat throughout, now work in patt from chart for Body as foll:

Work even until Back measures 16½in/42cm from cast-on edge, ending with RS facing for next row.

Shape armholes

Keeping patt correct, bind off 7 (8: 8: 9: 9) sts at beg of next 2 rows. 141 (145: 151: 155: 161) sts.**

Dec 1 st at each end of next 5 (5: 7: 7: 9) rows, then on foll 3 (4: 4: 5: 5) alt rows, then on 2 foll 4th rows. 121 (123: 125: 127: 129) sts.

Work even until armhole measures 9½ (9¾: 10¼: 10½: 11)in/24 (25: 26: 27: 28)cm, ending with RS facing for next row.

Shape shoulders and back neck

Bind off 11 sts at beg of next 2 rows. 99 (101: 103: 105: 107) sts.

Next row (RS) Bind off 11 sts, patt until there are 15 (16: 16: 16: 16) sts on right needle and turn, leaving rem sts on a holder.

Work each side of neck separately.

Bind off 4 sts at beg of next row.

Bind off rem 11 (12: 12: 12: 12) sts.

With RS facing, rejoin yarn to rem sts, bind off center 47 (47: 49: 51: 53) sts, patt to end.

Complete to match first side, reversing shapings.

FRONT

Work as given for Back to **.

Dec 1 st at each end of next 4 rows, ending with RS

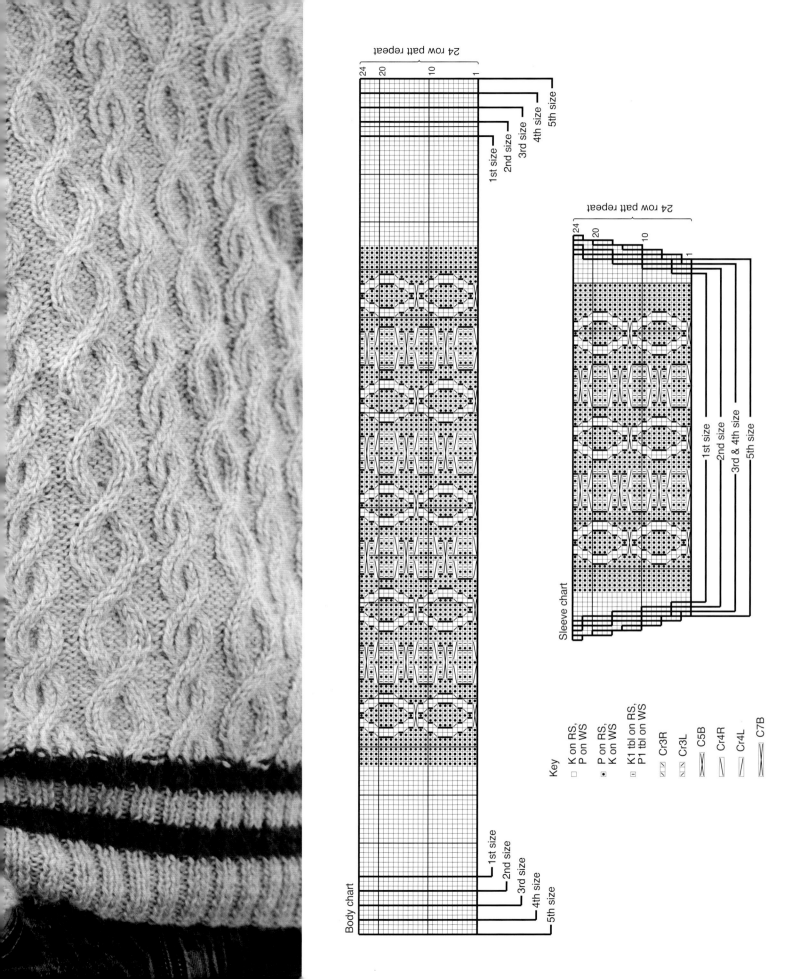

Body chart

24 row patt repeat

24 20 10 1

1st size
2nd size
3rd size
4th size
5th size

1st size
2nd size
3rd size
4th size
5th size

Sleeve chart

24 row patt repeat

24 20 10 1

1st size
2nd size
3rd & 4th size
5th size

Key

☐ K on RS, P on WS

■ P on RS, K on WS

⊡ K1 tbl on RS, P1 tbl on WS

Cr3R

Cr3L

C5B

Cr4R

Cr4L

C7B

facing for next row. 133 (137: 143: 147: 153) sts.

Divide for neck

Next row (RS) Work 2 tog, patt 64 (66: 69: 71: 74) sts and turn, leaving rem sts on a holder.

Work each side of neck separately.

Keeping patt correct, dec 1 st at armhole edge of 2nd (2nd: next: next: next) and foll 0 (0: 1: 1: 3) rows, then on foll 2 (3: 4: 5: 5) alt rows, then on 2 foll 4th rows **and at the same time** dec 1 st at neck edge of 2nd and every foll alt row. 53 sts.

Dec 1 st at neck edge **only** on 2nd and foll 18 (15: 15: 14: 14) alt rows, then on every foll 4th row until 33 (34: 34: 34: 34) sts rem.

Work even until Front matches Back to start of shoulder shaping, ending with RS facing for next row.

Shape shoulder

Bind off 11 sts at beg of next and foll alt row.

Work 1 row.

Bind off rem 11 (12: 12: 12: 12) sts.

With RS facing, slip center st onto a holder, rejoin yarn to rem sts, patt to last 2 sts, work 2 tog.

Complete to match first side, reversing shapings.

SLEEVES

Using size 3 (3.25mm) needles and MC, cast on 54 (56: 58: 58: 60) sts.

Row 1 (RS) P0 (1: 0: 0: 0), K2 (2: 0: 0: 1), *P2, K2; rep from * to last 0 (1: 2: 2: 3) sts, P0 (1: 2: 2: 2), K0 (0: 0: 0: 1).

Row 2 K0 (1: 0: 0: 0), P2 (2: 0: 0: 1), *K2, P2; rep from * to last 0 (1: 2: 2: 3) sts, K0 (1: 2: 2: 2), P0 (0: 0: 0: 1).

These 2 rows form rib.

Work as given for Back from *** to ***.

Row 30 (WS) Using A, rib 10 (11: 12: 12: 13), *[M1, rib 1] twice, M1, rib 4, [M1, rib 3] twice, M1, rib 4; rep from * once more, [M1, rib] twice, M1, rib to end. 69 (71: 73: 73: 75) sts.

Break off A and cont using MC only.

Change to size 6 (4mm) needles.

Starting and ending rows as indicated and repeating the 24 row patt repeat throughout, now work in patt from chart for Sleeve as foll:

Inc 1 st at each end of 5th (5th: 5th: 3rd: 3rd) and every foll 6th (6th: 6th: 4th: 4th) row until there are 99 (109: 107: 81: 81) sts, taking inc sts into St st.

1ST, 3RD, 4TH, AND 5TH SIZES ONLY

Inc 1 st at each end of every foll 8th (-: 8th: 6th: 6th) row

until there are 105 (-: 111: 115: 117) sts.

ALL SIZES

Work even until Sleeve measures 20½ (20½: 20¾: 20¾: 21¼)in/52 (52: 53: 53: 54)cm from cast-on edge, ending with RS facing for next row.

Shape top of sleeve

Keeping patt correct, bind off 7 (8: 8: 9: 9) sts at beg of next 2 rows. 91 (93: 95: 97: 99) sts.

Dec 1 st at each end of next 5 rows, then on foll 3 alt rows, then on every foll 4th row until 71 (73: 75: 77: 79) sts rem.

Work 1 row.

Dec 1 st at each end of next and every foll alt row until 57 sts rem, then on foll 11 rows, ending with RS facing for next row. 35 sts.

Bind off 4 sts at beg of next 2 rows.

Bind off rem 27 sts.

FINISHING

Press lightly on WS following instructions on yarn label.

Sew shoulder seams.

Neckband

With RS facing, using size 3 (3.25mm) circular needle and A, starting and ending at left shoulder seam, pick up and knit 72 (76: 80: 84: 88) sts down left side of neck, K st from holder at base of V and mark this st with a colored thread, pick up and knit 72 (76: 80: 84: 88) sts up right side of neck, then 42 (42: 42: 46: 46) sts from back. 187 (195: 203: 215: 223) sts.

Round 1 (RS) *K2, P2; rep from * to within 4 sts of marked st, K2, K2tog tbl, K marked st, K2tog, **K2, P2; rep from ** to end.

This round sets position of rib as given for Back.

Keeping rib correct as now set, cont as foll:

Round 2 Rib to within 2 sts of marked st, K2tog tbl, K marked st, K2tog, rib to end.

Rep last round 4 times more.

Join in MC.

Using MC, rep last round 6 times more.

Break off MC and cont using A only.

Rep last round 6 times more. 151 (159: 167: 179: 187) sts.

Bind off in rib, still decreasing either side of marker as before.

Sew side and sleeve seams. Sew sleeves into armholes.

STRIPED SCARF

Martin Storey

SIZE

The finished scarf measures 9½in/24cm by 71½in/182cm.

YARNS

5 x 50g/1¾oz balls of Rowan *RYC Cashsoft Aran* in **MC** (Thunder 014) and 1 ball each in **A** (Forest 018), **B** (Mole 003), **C** (Bud 006), and **D** (Burst 005)

NEEDLES

Pair of size 7 (4.5mm) knitting needles

GAUGE

19 sts and 36 rows to 4in/10cm measured over garter st using size 7 (4.5mm) needles *or size to obtain correct gauge.*

ABBREVIATIONS

See page 133.

SCARF

First section

Using size 7 (4.5mm) needles and A, cast on 46 sts.
Working in garter st throughout and joining in and breaking off colors as required, cont as foll:
Using A work 8 rows.
Using MC work 12 rows.
Using C work 2 rows.
Using MC work 12 rows.
Rep last 14 rows once more.
Using C work 2 rows.
Using MC work 4 rows.
Rep last 6 rows 3 times more.
Using A work 8 rows.
Using MC work 16 rows.
Rep last 24 rows 6 times more.
Using C work 2 rows.
Using MC work 4 rows.

Rep last 6 rows until First Section measures 35¾in/91cm, ending after a WS row using MC.**
Break off yarn and leave sts on a holder.

Second Section

Work as given for First Section to **, **but** using B in place of A and D in place of C.

Join sections

Holding RS of First Section against RS of Second Section, bind off both sets of sts at same time, taking one st from one section with corresponding st of other section.

FINISHING

Do NOT press.

PLAIN JACKET

Martin Storey

To fit chest

40	42	44	46	48	in
102	107	112	117	122	cm

Finished measurements

AROUND CHEST

47½	49¼	52	53½	56	in
121	125	132	136	142	cm

LENGTH TO BACK NECK

26	26½	26¾	27	27½	in
66	67	68	69	70	cm

SLEEVE SEAM

20½	20½	20¾	20¾	21¼	in
52	52	53	53	54	cm

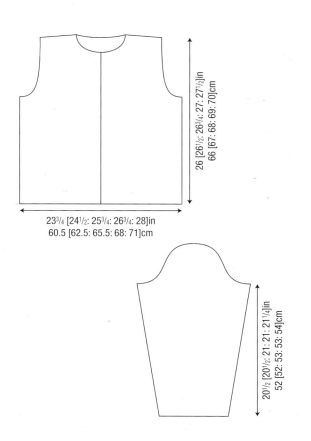

26 [26½: 26¾: 27: 27½]in
66 [67: 68: 69: 70]cm

23¾ [24½: 25¾: 26¾: 28]in
60.5 [62.5: 65.5: 68: 71]cm

20½ [20½: 21: 21: 21¼]in
52 [52: 53: 53: 54]cm

YARNS

18 (19: 20: 21: 22) x 50g/1¾oz balls of *Rowan RYC Cashsoft Aran* in Mole 003

NEEDLES

Pair of size 6 (4mm) knitting needles
Pair of size 7 (4.5mm) knitting needles

EXTRAS

5 buttons

GAUGE

19 sts and 25 rows to 4in/10cm measured over St st using size 7 (4.5mm) needles *or size to obtain correct gauge.*

ABBREVIATIONS

See page 133.

BACK

Using size 6 (4mm) needles, cast on 115 (119: 125: 129: 135) sts.
Row 1 (RS) P0 (1: 0: 0: 0), K2 (3: 1: 3: 0), *P3, K3; rep from * to last 5 (1: 4: 0: 3) sts, P3 (1: 3: 0: 3), K2 (0: 1: 0: 0).
Row 2 K0 (1: 0: 0: 0), P2 (3: 1: 3: 0), *K3, P3; rep from * to last 5 (1: 4: 0: 3) sts, K3 (1: 3: 0: 3), P2 (0: 1: 0: 0).
These 2 rows form rib.
Work in rib for 20 rows more, ending with RS facing for next row.
Change to size 7 (4.5mm) needles.
Starting with a K row, work in St st until Back measures 16½in/42cm from cast-on edge, ending with RS facing for next row.
Shape armholes
Bind off 6 (7: 7: 8: 8) sts at beg of next 2 rows. 103 (105: 111: 113: 119) sts.
Dec 1 st at each end of next 5 (5: 7: 7: 9) rows, then on foll 3 alt rows, then on foll 4th row. 85 (87: 89: 91: 93) sts.
Work even until armhole measures 9½ (9¾: 10¼: 10½: 11)in/24 (25: 26: 27: 28)cm, ending with RS facing for next row.
Shape shoulders and back neck
Bind off 8 (9: 9: 9: 9) sts at beg of next 2 rows. 69 (69: 71: 73: 75) sts.

Next row (RS) Bind off 8 (9: 9: 9: 9) sts, K until there are 13 (12: 12: 12: 12) sts on right needle and turn, leaving rem sts on a holder.
Work each side of neck separately.
Bind off 4 sts at beg of next row.
Bind off rem 9 (8: 8: 8: 8) sts.
With RS facing, rejoin yarn to rem sts, bind off center 27 (27: 29: 31: 33) sts, K to end.
Complete to match first side, reversing shapings.

LEFT FRONT

Using size 6 (4mm) needles, cast on 58 (60: 63: 65: 68) sts.
Row 1 (RS) P0 (1: 0: 0: 0), K2 (3: 1: 3: 0), *P3, K3; rep from * to last 2 sts, P2.
Row 2 K2, P3, *K3, P3; rep from * to last 5 (1: 4: 0: 3) sts, K3 (1: 3: 0: 3), P2 (0: 1: 0: 0).
These 2 rows form rib.
Work in rib for 20 rows more, ending with RS facing for next row.
Change to size 7 (4.5mm) needles.
Starting with a K row, work in St st for 12 rows, ending with RS facing for next row.
Place pocket
Next row (RS) K20 and turn, leaving rem 38 (40: 43: 45: 48) sts on a holder.
Cast on 28 sts (for pocket back) at beg of next row. 48 sts.
Work 34 rows on these 48 sts for pocket back and side front, ending with RS facing for next row.
Next row (RS) K20, bind off rem 28 sts.
Break off yarn and leave sts on another holder.
Return to 38 (40: 43: 45: 48) sts left on first holder and rejoin yarn with RS facing.
Work 37 rows on these sts for pocket front, ending with WS facing for next row.
Join sections
Next row (WS) P across 38 (40: 43: 45: 48) sts of pocket front, then P across 20 sts left on second holder. 58 (60: 63: 65: 68) sts.
Work even until Left Front matches Back to start of armhole shaping, ending with RS facing for next row.
Shape armhole
Bind off 6 (7: 7: 8: 8) sts at beg of next row. 52 (53: 56: 57: 60) sts.
Work 1 row.

Dec 1 st at armhole edge of next
5 (5: 7: 7: 9) rows, then on foll 3 alt
rows, then on foll 4th row. 43 (44:
45: 46: 47) sts.
Work even until 15 (17: 17: 17: 19)
rows less have been worked than
on Back to start of shoulder
shaping, ending with WS facing for
next row.

Shape neck

Bind off 10 (9: 10: 11: 11) sts at beg
of next row. 33 (35: 35: 35: 36) sts.
Dec 1 st at neck edge of next
5 rows, then on 2 (3: 3: 3: 4) alt
rows, then on foll 4th row. 25 (26:
26: 26: 26) sts.
Work 1 row, ending with RS facing
for next row.

Shape shoulder

Bind off 8 (9: 9: 9: 9) sts at beg of
next and foll alt row.
Work 1 row.
Bind off rem 9 (8: 8: 8: 8) sts.

RIGHT FRONT

Using size 6 (4mm) needles, cast on
58 (60: 63: 65: 68) sts.
Row 1 (RS) P2, K3, *P3, K3; rep
from * to last 5 (1: 4: 0: 3) sts, P3 (1:
3: 0: 3), K2 (0: 1: 0: 0).
Row 2 K0 (1: 0: 0: 0), P2 (3: 1: 3: 0),
*K3, P3; rep from * to last 2 sts, K2.
These 2 rows form rib.
Work in rib for 20 rows more,
ending with RS facing for next row.
Change to size 7 (4.5mm) needles.
Starting with a K row, work in St st
for 12 rows, ending with RS facing
for next row.

Place pocket

Next row (RS) K38 (40: 43: 45: 48)
and turn, leaving rem 20 sts on a
holder.
Work 37 rows on these sts for
pocket front, ending with WS facing
for next row.

Break off yarn and leave sts on another holder.

Return to 20 sts left on first holder, rejoin yarn with RS facing, cast on 28 sts (for pocket back), K to end. 48 sts.

Work 35 rows on these 48 sts for pocket back and side front, ending with RS facing for next row.

Next row (RS) Bind off 28 sts, K to end. 20 sts.

Join sections

Next row (WS) P across 20 sts of side front, then P across 38 (40: 43: 45: 48) sts left on second holder. 58 (60: 63: 65: 68) sts.

Complete to match Left Front, reversing shapings.

SLEEVES

Using size 6 (4mm) needles, cast on 47 (49: 51: 51: 53) sts.

Row 1 (RS) P1 (2: 0: 0: 0), K3 (3: 0: 0: 1), *P3, K3; rep from * to last 1 (2: 3: 3: 4) sts, P1 (2: 3: 3: 3), K0 (0: 0: 0: 1).

Row 2 K1 (2: 0: 0: 0), P3 (3: 0: 0: 1), *K3, P3; rep from * to last 1 (2: 3: 3: 4) sts, K1 (2: 3: 3: 3), P0 (0: 0: 0: 1).
These 2 rows form rib.

Work in rib for 20 rows more, ending with RS facing for next row.

Change to size 7 (4.5mm) needles.

Starting with a K row, work in St st, shaping sides by inc 1 st at each end of 5th (5th: 5th: 4th: 5th) and every foll 6th row until there are 77 (79: 79: 85: 87) sts.

1ST, 2ND, AND 3RD SIZES ONLY

Inc 1 st at each end of every foll 8th row until there are 79 (81: 83: -: -) sts.

ALL SIZES

Work even until Sleeve measures 20½ (20½: 20¾: 20¾: 21¼)in/52 (52: 53: 53: 54)cm from cast-on edge, ending with RS facing for next row.

Shape top of sleeve

Bind off 6 (7: 7: 8: 8) sts at beg of next 2 rows. 67 (67: 69: 69: 71) sts.

Dec 1 st at each end of next 5 rows, then on foll 3 alt rows, then on every foll 4th row until 45 (45: 47: 47: 49) sts rem.

Work 1 row.

Dec 1 st at each end of next and every foll alt row until 35 sts rem, then on foll 3 rows, ending with RS facing for next row. 29 sts.

Bind off 5 sts at beg of next 2 rows.

Bind off rem 19 sts.

FINISHING

Press lightly on WS following instructions on yarn label. Sew shoulder seams.

Collar

With RS facing and using size 6 (4mm) needles, starting and ending at front opening edges, pick up and knit 32 (35: 34: 34: 36) sts up right side of neck, 35 (35: 37: 37: 39) sts from back, then 32 (35: 34: 34: 36) sts down left side of neck. 99 (105: 105: 105: 111) sts.

Row 1 (RS of Collar, WS of Front) K3, *P3, K3; rep from * to end.

Row 2 P3, *K3, P3; rep from * to end.

These 2 rows form rib.

Work in rib until Collar measures 4¾in/12cm from pick-up row.

Bind off in rib.

Button band

With RS facing and using size 6 (4mm) needles, starting at cast-on edge, pick up and knit 131 (131: 131: 137: 137) sts evenly up right front opening edge to Collar pick-up row.

Row 1 (WS) K1, P3, *K3, P3; rep from * to last st, K1.

Row 2 K4, *P3, K3; rep from * to last st, K1.

These 2 rows form rib.

Work in rib for 6 rows more, ending with WS facing for next row.

Bind off in rib (on WS).

Buttonhole band

With RS facing and using size 6 (4mm) needles, starting at Collar pick-up row, pick up and knit 131 (131: 131: 137: 137) sts evenly down left front opening edge to cast-on edge.

Work in rib as given for Button Band for 3 rows, ending with RS facing for next row.

Row 4 (RS) Rib 24 (24: 24: 26: 26), *work 2 tog, yo (to make a buttonhole), rib 23 (23: 23: 24: 24); rep from * 3 times more, work 2 tog, yo (to make 5th buttonhole), rib 5.

Work in rib for 4 rows more, ending with WS facing for next row.

Bind off in rib (on WS).

Collar bands (both alike)

With RS of Collar (WS of body) facing and using size 6 (4mm) needles, pick up and knit 29 sts evenly row-end edge of Collar, between pick-up row and bound-off edge.

Work in rib as given for Button Band for 8 rows, ending with WS facing for next row.

Bind off in rib (on WS).

Sew row-end edges of Collar Bands to row-end edges of front bands level with collar pick-up row.

Pocket bands (both alike)

With RS facing and using size 6 (4mm) needles, pick up and knit 35 sts evenly row-end edge of pocket opening.

Work in rib as given for Button Band for 8 rows, ending with WS facing for next row.

Bind off in rib (on WS).

Sew pocket linings in place on inside, then neatly sew down ends of pocket bands. Sew sleeves into armholes. Sew side and sleeve seams. Sew on buttons.

The following notes will help you knit the garments in this book successfully.

GAUGE

Obtaining the correct gauge is the factor that can make the difference between a garment that fits and one that does not. It controls both the shape and size of a knitted garment, so any variation, however slight, can distort the finished size. Different designers feature in this book and it is their gauge, given at the start of each pattern, that you must match.

To check this against your own gauge, we recommend that you knit a square in pattern and/or stockinette stitch (depending on the pattern instructions) of about 5 to 10 more stitches and 5 to 10 more rows than those given in the gauge note. Mark the central 4 inches (10cm) square with pins. If you have too many stitches to 4 inches (10cm), try again using a larger needle size. If you have too few stitches to 10cm (4in), try again using a smaller needle size.

Once you have achieved the correct gauge, your garment will be knitted to the measurements indicated in the size diagram shown with the pattern.

SIZING

The instructions in each pattern are given for the smallest size. The figures in parentheses are for the larger sizes. Where there is one set of figures only, it applies to all sizes.

All garment patterns include "ease" to allow for a comfortable fit. The finished measurement around the bust/chest of the knitted garment is given at the start of each pattern and includes this ease. The size diagram shows the finished width of the garment at the underarm, and it is this measurement that you should use to choose an appropriate size.

A useful tip is to measure one of your own garments that fits comfortably and choose a size that is similar.

Having chosen a size based on width, look at the corresponding length for that size; if you are not happy with the total length that we recommend, adjust your own garment before beginning your armhole shaping—any adjustment after this point will mean that your sleeve will not fit into your garment easily; and don't forget to take your adjustment into account if there is any side-seam shaping.

Finally, look at the sleeve length; the size diagram shows the finished sleeve measurement, taking into account any top-arm insertion length. Measure your body between the center of your neck and your wrist, this measurement should correspond to half the garment width plus the sleeve length. Again, your sleeve length may be adjusted, but remember to take into consideration your sleeve increases if you do adjust the length—you must increase more frequently than the pattern states to shorten your sleeve, less frequently to lengthen it.

CHART NOTE

Many of the patterns in the book are worked from charts. Each square on a chart represents a stitch and each line of squares represents a row of knitting. Each color used is given a different letter and these are shown in the materials section, or in the key alongside the chart of each pattern.

When working from the charts, read odd-numbered rows (K) from right to left and even-numbered rows (P) from left to right, unless stated otherwise.

KNITTING WITH MORE THAN ONE COLOR

There are two main methods of working color into a knitted fabric: the intarsia and Fair Isle techniques. The first method produces a single thickness of fabric and is usually used where a color is only required in a particular area of a row. Where a repeating pattern is created across the row, the Fair Isle technique is usually used.

Intarsia technique

For this technique, cut lengths of yarn for each motif or block of color used in a row. Then join in the various colors at the appropriate position in the row, linking one color to the next by twisting them around each other where they meet on the wrong side to avoid gaps.

All yarn ends can then either be darned along the color join lines after each motif is completed, or can be "knitted-in" on the wrong side of the knitting as each color is worked into the pattern. This is done in much the same way as "weaving-in" yarns when working the Fair Isle technique and saves time darning-in ends.

It is essential that the gauge is noted for intarsia, because this may vary from the plain stockinette stitch gauge if both are used in the same pattern.

Fair Isle technique

When two or three colors are worked repeatedly across a row, strand the yarn not in use loosely behind the stitches being worked.

If you are working with more than two colors, treat the "floating" yarns as if they were one yarn and always spread the stitches to their correct width to keep them elastic.

It is advisable not to carry the stranded or "floating" yarns over more than three stitches at a time, but to weave them under and over the color you are working to catch the "floating" yarns into the back of the work.

SLIP-STITCH EDGINGS

When a row end edge forms the actual finished edge of a garment or an accessory like a scarf, a slip-stitch edging makes a neat edge.

To work a slip-stitch edging at the end of a right side row, work across the row until there is one stitch left on the left needle. Pick up the loop lying between the needles and place this loop on the right needle. (Note that this loop does NOT count as a stitch and is not included in any stitch counts.) Now slip the last stitch knitwise with the yarn at the back of the work. At the beginning of the next row, purl together the first (slipped) stitch with the picked-up loop.

To work a slip-stitch edging at the end of a wrong side row, work across the row until there is one stitch left on the left needle. Pick up the loop lying between the needles and place this loop on the right needle.

(Note that this loop does NOT count as a stitch and is not included in any stitch counts.) Now slip the last stitch purlwise with the yarn at the front of the work. At the beginning of the next row, knit together through the back of the loop the first (slipped) stitch with the picked-up loop.

FINISHING INSTRUCTIONS

After you have worked for hours knitting a garment, it would be a pity to spoil it by not taking enough care with the pressing and finishing process. Follow these tips for a truly professional-looking garment.

PRESSING

Block out each piece of knitting and, following the instructions on the yarn label, press the garment pieces, avoiding any ribbing.

Take special care to press the edges, as this will make sewing the seams both easier and neater. If the yarn label indicates that the fabric should not be pressed, then covering the blocked out fabric with a damp white cotton cloth and leaving it to stand will have the desired effect.

Darn in all ends neatly along the selvage edge or a color join, as appropriate.

SEWING SEAMS

When sewing the pieces together, remember to match areas of color and texture very carefully where they meet. Use backstitch or mattress stitch for all main knitting seams, and sew together ribbing and neckband seams with mattress stitch, unless stated otherwise.

CONSTRUCTION

Having completed the garment pieces, sew the seams in the order stated in the instructions. After sewing the shoulder seams, sew the top of the sleeve to the body of the garment using the method detailed in the pattern, referring to the appropriate guide:

Straight bound-off sleeves: Place the center of the bound-off edge of the sleeve at the shoulder seam. Sew the top of the sleeve to the back and front.

Square set-in sleeves: Place the center of the bound-off edge of the sleeve at the shoulder seam. Sew the top of the sleeve into the armhole, with the straight sides at the top of the sleeve forming a neat right-angle to the bound-off stitches at the armhole.

Shallow set-in sleeves: Place the center of the bound-off edge of the sleeve at the shoulder seam. Match the decreases at the beginning of the armhole shaping with the decreases at the top of the sleeve, and sew the sleeve cap to the armhole, easing in the shapings.

Set-in sleeves: Place the center of the bound-off edge of the sleeve at the shoulder seam. Sew in the sleeve, easing the sleeve cap into the armhole.

Lastly, slip stitch any pocket edgings and linings in place and sew on buttons to correspond with buttonholes.

KNITTING ABBREVIATIONS

The following are the standard knitting abbreviations used in this book. Any special abbreviations (such as those for cables) are given at the beginning of individual patterns.

alt	alternate
beg	begin(ning)
cm	centimeter(s)
cont	continu(e)(ing)
dec	decreas(e)(ing)
DK	double knitting (a lightweight to medium-weight yarn)
foll	follow(s)(ing)
garter st	garter stitch (K every row)
in	inch(es)
inc	increas(e)(ing)
inc 1	increase one st by working into front and back of stitch
K	knit
K2tog	knit next 2 sts together
m	meter(s)
M1	make one stitch by picking up horizontal loop before next stitch and knitting into back of it
MC	main color (of yarn)
mm	millimeter(s)
P	purl
P2tog	purl next 2 sts together
patt	pattern; *or* work in pattern
psso	pass slipped stitch over

rem	remain(s)(ing)
rep	repeat(ing)
rev St st	reverse stockinette stitch (P all RS rows and K all WS rows)
RS	right side
sl	slip
st(s)	stitch(es)
St st	stockinette stitch (K all RS rows and P all WS rows)
tbl	through back of loop(s)
tog	together
WS	wrong side
yd	yard(s)
yo	yarn over right needle to make a new stitch

0	no stitches, times or rows for that size
–	instructions do not apply to this size
*	Repeat instructions after asterick or between asterisks as many times as instructed.
[ ]	Repeat instructions inside brackets as many times as instructed.

ABOUT THE YARNS

The following yarns are used in this book. For the best results, use the yarn specified in the knitting pattern. All yarn information was correct at the time of publication, but yarn companies change their products frequently and cannot absolutely guarantee that yarn types or shades will be available when you come to use these patterns. The yarn descriptions will help you find a substitute if necessary. When substituting yarns, always check that the gauge and the ball length are similar.

Rowan Felted Tweed
A lightweight yarn; 50% merino wool, 25% alpaca, 25% viscose/rayon; approximately 191yd/175m per 50g/1¾oz ball; recommended gauge—22–24 sts and 30–32 rows to 4in/10cm measured over St st using size 5–6 (3.75–4mm) needles.

Rowan Pure Wool DK
A lightweight 100% super-wash wool yarn; approximately 137yd/125m per 50g/1¾oz ball; recommended gauge—22 sts and 30 rows to 4in/10cm measured over St st using size 6 (4mm) needles.

Rowan RYC Baby Alpaca DK
A lightweight 100% pure alpaca yarn; approximately 109yd/100m per 50g/1¾oz ball; recommended gauge—22 sts and 30 rows to 4in/10cm measured over St st using size 6 (4mm) needles.

Rowan RYC Cashsoft Aran
A medium-weight yarn; 57% merino wool, 33% microfiber, 10% cashmere; approximately 95yd/87m per 50g/1¾/4oz ball; recommended gauge—19 sts and 25 rows to 4in/10cm measured over St st using size 7 (4.5mm) needles.

Rowan RYC Cashsoft DK
A lightweight yarn; 57% merino wool, 33% microfiber, 10% cashmere; approximately 142yd/130m per 50g/1¾oz ball; recommended gauge—22 sts and 30 rows to 4in/10cm measured over St st using size 6 (4mm) needles.

Rowan Scottish Tweed Aran
A medium-weight 100% pure wool yarn; approximately 186yd/170m per 100g/3½oz ball; recommended gauge—16 sts and 23 rows to 4in/10cm measured over St st using size 8–9 (5–5.5mm) needles.

Rowan Scottish Tweed Chunky
A bulky-weight 100% pure wool yarn; approximately 109yd/100m per 100g/3½oz ball; recommended gauge—12 sts and 16 rows to 4in/10cm measured over St st using size 11 (8mm) needles.

Rowan Scottish Tweed DK
A lightweight 100% pure wool yarn; approximately 123yd/113m per 50g/1¾oz ball; recommended gauge—20–22 sts and 28–30 rows to 4in/10cm measured over St st using size 6 (4mm) needles.

Rowan Scottish Tweed 4 ply
A fine-weight 100% pure wool yarn; approximately 120yd/110m per 25g/⅞oz ball; recommended gauge—26–28 sts and 38–40 rows to 4in/10cm measured over St st using size 2–3 (3–3.25mm) needles.

Rowan Wool Cotton
A lightweight yarn; 50 % merino wool, 50% cotton; approximately 123yd/113m per 50g/1¾oz ball; recommended gauge—22–24 sts and 30–32 rows to 4in/10cm measured over St st using size 5–6 (3.75–4mm) needles.